Love ♡
HardER

International Bestselling Author
MONICA JAMES

Copyrighted Material
LOVE HARDER

This book is a work of fiction. Names, characters, places, and incidents are the product of the author's imagination, or are used fictitiously. Any resemblance to actual events, locales, or persons living or dead, is coincidental. Any trademarks, service marks, product names or named features are assumed to be the property of their respective owners and are used only for reference.

Copyright © 2024 by Monica James

All rights reserved. No part of this work may be reproduced, scanned or distributed in any printed or electronic form without the express, written consent of the author.

Cover Models: Monica & Darby
Photographer: Michelle Lancaster
Editing: Editing 4 Indies

Interior Design and Formatting by

E.M. TIPPETTS

E.M. Tippetts Book Designs

Follow me on:
authormonicajames.com

Other Books By
MONICA JAMES

THE I SURRENDER SERIES
I Surrender
Surrender to Me
Surrendered
White

SOMETHING LIKE NORMAL SERIES
Something like Normal
Something like Redemption
Something like Love

A HARD LOVE ROMANCE
Dirty Dix
Wicked Dix
The Hunt

MEMORIES FROM YESTERDAY DUET
Forgetting You, Forgetting Me
Forgetting You, Remembering Me

SINS OF THE HEART DUET
Absinthe of the Heart
Defiance of the Heart

ALL THE PRETTY THINGS TRILOGY
Bad Saint
Fallen Saint
Forever My Saint
The Devil's Crown-Part One (Spin-Off)
The Devil's Crown-Part Two (Spin-Off)

THE MONSTERS WITHIN DUET
Bullseye
Blowback

DELIVER US FROM EVIL TRILOGY
Thy Kingdom Come
Into Temptation
Deliver Us From Evil

IN LOVE AND WAR
North of the Stars
Fall of the Stars

REVENGE IS SWEET SERIES
Crybaby

HEART MEMORY TRANSFER DUET
Heart Sick
Love Sick

STANDALONE
Mr. Write
Chase the Butterflies
Beyond the Roses
Someone Else's Shadow
Love Hard
Love Harder

This book is dedicated to love—how I hate to love you…

Preface

This memoir is a work of creative nonfiction.
While all persons and the situations the author writes about are inspired, in part, by real people and events, no names are used to protect the innocent… and the guilty.
Certain events have been fictionalized. The conversations are not a word-for-word retelling because a lot of gin was consumed. This is how the author remembers things…she thinks.
The author is a lover, not a fighter, so don't come at her. She knows she has made some really stupid decisions throughout her life—you'll soon see.
She thanks you for not looking at her with judgy eyes.
This is not a story of the author's life. But rather, it's a story about life.
Happy reading, and Godspeed…

GIRLS!
GIRLS JUST WANNA have FUN!
OMG!
Strong girls
believe
Oh la laaa...

LOVE

LOVE
O
V
E

Four simple letters which, on their own, are hardly remarkable. But strung together…they have the ability to fuck you, and fuck you hard without buying you dinner first.

Why do we put our trust, our faith, in a stranger? Because of…love? Are we all just hopeless romantics at heart, chasing the proverbial happily ever after?

Once upon a time, I looked at love through rose-tinted glasses because love is meant to conquer all, right? Love was the reason Romeo drank the poison, why Bella sparkled, and why Jack froze to death as Rose sprawled out comfortably on a door big enough for ten and caught some zzz's.

Being a romance writer, one may think I have my shit sorted when it comes to love.

I hate to spoil the ending for you, dear reader, but love and me, we aren't friends. We haven't been for quite some time. And that's not because I don't believe in love.

On the contrary.

I love love…but it seems love doesn't love me. Or perhaps love is a sadistic bitch that enjoys giving me a taste of what I want, only to blow me a raspberry and sing na nah na na nah.

I am no one special.

I am someone who wakes every single morning and appreciates everything she has. These voices inside my head have been my saving grace in a way. I write to deal with my pain. I write to help myself heal. I write to survive because some days are a struggle.

Some good.

Some bad.

But all in all, I'm just like you.

I laugh.

I cry.

And I love.

There's one thing my friends know to be true: when I love, I love hard. There's no in-between. I don't love easily because, like every single human being on this planet, I've been hurt. Been hurt to the point of losing parts of myself that I'll never be able to get back.

I see these losses as character-building, a lesson learned, but that doesn't mean it lessens the pain. Or that it doesn't fucking suck.

My experiences with life and love are the reason I write, and I'm fortunate enough to have readers from all over the world connecting with my words. Whether it's one book, one chapter, or one page, I never take for granted that something I created resonates with people.

It blows my mind.

And that's what brings me to the now.

Buckle up, bestie. Things are about to get wild.

I wanted to write something different because, like all my story ideas, this idea wouldn't let me sleep. It wouldn't let me breathe without thinking about… *him.*

Love♡HardER

We all have a him.

A her.

A person in our lives who gives us hope that there is more to life than… this.

For me, that person caught me unawares because I wasn't looking both ways when crossing the street, and that's when life best throws you a curveball and screams KEEP UP! And most times, we can't. We're thrown into the deep end without a life vest and expected to swim through the currents that are sure to drown us.

Love and I were on a sabbatical, ETA unknown. And I was happy with that reality. If you've read *LOVE HARD*, you know that love and I were no longer on speaking terms.

I have always been a solitary being. It comes with the job, I guess. But even before writing, I always enjoyed the silence more than the noise. I took solace in simplicity because it's where beauty truly shines.

I survived a failed marriage and a rekindled love that should have never been relit.

I don't regret my time with these men, but would I have done things differently? The answer is hell to the fuck yes. But the thing about hindsight is that it's fucking useless. I don't look back and regret my choices because, at the time, those choices were the right ones to make.

Did I learn from them?

Probably not.

But the one thing I did learn is that I am a lot stronger than I ever gave myself credit for. I learned that I don't need a man to complete me. I don't need another person to validate my existence because, in the end, I'm the one who has to live with my choices.

That's progress, right?

So I should have known better when *he* swept me off my feet…only to throw me off a cliff and watch me drown.

I fell for him, and boy, did I fall hard.

He was everything I wanted—looks, personality, heart; he was the perfect package. However, perfect doesn't exist. I knew this. Yet I allowed him in when I should have slammed the door in his face.

Dating today is a fucking dumpster fire rolling down a hill while attempting to avoid a gauntlet of deathtraps along the way.

Swipe left.

Swipe right.

Love me.

Love me not.

I cannot keep up.

We live in a disposable world where one doesn't even have to leave the house anymore to "meet" people. It's all within a swipe to decide whether your "true love" is really out there.

I really miss the good old days when one's ex stayed dead and buried and you never had to see or hear from them again. Now, it seems social media likes to recommend "friends" one may want to connect with.

Heads-up, they're not on my friends list for a reason.

I don't care what they're doing. Who they're fucking, and if she loved the Boston Pancake he gave her for their one-month anniversary (you're welcome, Blush Podcast Besties). And I don't care what they ate for dinner (here's hoping it's not an Alabama Tuna Melt. Again, Blush Besties, we will discuss further).

I choose not to see because ignorance is truly bliss.

You know what my triggers are…life. Life triggers me daily.

I'm all about my nurturing inner peace these days, and anything that disturbs that peace can fuck right off and take itself out with the trash I left outside. But social media seems to enjoy rubbing salt in the wounds of the brokenhearted any chance it gets, which is why I decided to write a book about dating in the modern world.

Whoever thought this was a good idea was clearly on crack, but alas, here we are.

The idea was called 40 Dates, 40 Nights, and I proposed to do just that. Who am I to back down from a challenge, no matter how insane it may be? I thought it was a clever play on the biblical coined phrase because this was, without a doubt, going to be a nightmare of biblical proportions.

I wanted to write a book about online dating versus IRL dating. I hate that that acronym exists, but it seems we're even too lazy to speak words nowadays and would rather use abbreviations because it's all about the hustle, baby.

I learned so much while researching. Some things I wish I could burn from my mind with a blowtorch. Others were rather educational.

I have always been fascinated by humans.

Every single one of us is different in our own way, and those ways are paths I enjoy traveling along, especially when I find a human who challenges me in ways I haven't been before. Honestly, the weirder, the better.

I don't use that term in a derogatory light because I am a proud weirdo. I have always gravitated toward the macabre. The strange. There is so much more to life…we just have to know where to look. Or get lost while searching.

I have surrounded myself with a group of misfits who are the most beautiful weirdos I love with my entire heart. They give me hope that good people do exist. Without my weirdos, I wouldn't be here. That's no word of a lie.

So embrace your tribe because they are the ones who will be your light when the darkness threatens to siphon out your flame. My girls and I have laughed; we've cried over the men in our lives. We've given nicknames to the men who love bombed us for weeks and promised they were different, only to be lying a-holes, faster than they can "root and boot" because if you can't laugh, you'll cry, right?

(I love you, Bunny, Angel, Mötley, and Sparkles).

Our conversation would go along the lines of, "How's Maraca?"

"Maraca? You mean Chicken Skin?"

"Chicken Skin? Was he the one with the balloon dick?"

"Balloon dick? You mean, the one who howled like a hyena when he came?"

"Hmm…that's Tiny Nipples."

"Oh shit, that's right. Maybe he and Leprechaun can dance under the rainbow together in their velour tracksuits."

For the record, we do not condone the ridiculing of any decent human being, but these men were not decent, and they totally deserved it.

I've never settled in life. I've always looked for the exceptional because that's what I want. That's what I deserve. As clichéd as it is, life is too short to settle for anything less. Even in past relationships, they were exceptional enough for me to commit at the time.

Although they didn't work, it doesn't lessen their impact on my life. I connected with them and learned a lot. To connect with a human being is a remarkable thing. It's rare, but it changes your world forevermore when it happens.

So I went into writing a book about modern-day dating with the same mindset. I wanted to connect with someone who inspired me enough to want to write about them.

Best idea…said no one ever.

It seems not only am I stubborn and fussy, but I'm also old-school because the moment a guy asked if I wanted to see his dick, I succumbed to the pressure of society and hit that unmatch button faster than I could scream what in the ever-living donkey dick fuck?

Why do people think it's common practice to send an unsolicited dick pic? Or even a tit pic?

This behavior is frowned upon in public, so why is it an acceptable online practice? It seems hiding behind a screen name has given many a false bravado where they think it's okay to behave in such a manner online. Whereas, in real life, one could be arrested for freeing Willy.

The line blurs with online dating because one has no repercussions for their actions. They think behaving a certain way is okay because no one can see them. No one knows who they truly are. They can remain incognito, forever hiding beneath the *Harry Potter* invisibility cloak while sending random people pictures of their pink bits.

What's the worst that can happen?

Well, the worst that can happen is this memoir because your beloved narrator fell for someone. Actually, she fell for more than one someone. And damn, did she fall hard. She fell so hard for one man in particular, she thought he could possibly be "the one."

He promised me he was different, only to be worse than anyone ever before him. I told him what broke me, only for him to break me even more.

But you see, our man of the hour, he thought he could ghost me… Well, he thought wrong.

GHOST

G<i>hosting.</i>
Another term coined by online dating.

Most know what ghosting is, but for those viewers at home who don't, ghosting is another word for a man or woman being a fucking coward. They'd rather not have an adult conversation and be honest. Or maybe they're just a lying asshole who, once they've had their fun, show their true colors, and that color is bullshit.

All in all, ghosting someone is when someone cuts off contact with someone without giving said person any warning or explanation for the silence. The ghostee feels powerless because they aren't given the opportunity to express their feelings to the ghoster, aka the chickenshit.

It is emotionally cruel because it is done with intent.

The ghostee is then left with questions that, in most cases, remain unanswered, and therefore, this experience may trickle into future relationships and cause trust issues because once a ghostee, always a ghostee.

How do I know so much about ghosting?

Well, I'm a ghostee.

Shock.

Horror.

I know.

I should know better.

But clearly, I don't.

And that's why I wanted to write this book because ghosting happens far too often. I cannot believe the number of people I've spoken to whose story reflects mine. How many broken hearts are out there because of ghosting.

Shall we go back to the day it began?

It all started with a wonderful dating app.

Don't shake your head at me. I know, I know. But it started for research purposes, and I promised myself I wouldn't get hooked.

For those of you who aren't familiar with dating apps, they're all pretty much the same—window-shopping but for humans. Humans for a night or humans for a lifetime—it's your call. Those who scroll through the endless photos of strangers are looking for someone to vibe with. Someone to talk to. Or someone to fuck.

The dating world is truly at your fingertips, and whatever you're in the mood for can be delivered to your door. Very much like ordering junk food via Uber Eats at midnight might satisfy the cravings. It's convenient, quick, and easy, but come morning, you'll regret that midnight snack because you know it isn't good for you. It leaves you feeling like crap and questioning whether you should go vegan instead.

We can be *that* fussy because if someone doesn't match your height requirement or you're not vibing with their latest threads, then it's a swipe left for your next potential human.

It's that simple and shallow, I'm afraid.

For me, any man holding a fish, had smudgy photos because his camera was covered in a film of filth, or if I had to decipher who he actually was as all his photos were of him and "the boys," then it was a no deal for me. I want simple, sanitary, and originality. None of these things are that.

I found a few interesting men who inspired me to write. I wish there were a formula. But there isn't. I just know when I'm inspired, and when I am, I act. Most men were apprehensive about being "studied," and I could not blame them.

However, some were interested and provided great insight. I didn't get attached because I was there with a purpose.

There's one thing I should mention—I am not perfect in any way, shape, or form. Who would have guessed, right? I would rather self-sabotage love than be broken by it. I wish it got easier the older you get, but for me, anyway, it hasn't.

So this is the mindset I have whenever I meet someone new.

This is why I felt I could write a book about dating and not get attached. I wasn't here to catch feelings. I was here to write and hoped my experiences resonated with others.

Nothing was eventful about the day I matched with him.

I didn't wake and feel like something monumental was about to occur. And that's when most things do. It's the things that catch you unawares that leave a lasting impact.

Like he did.

His name?

Let's just call him Ghost.

I was scrolling through my likes and looking for that something, something. After a while, each face kind of morphs into one, and it's only when my spidey senses start tingling do I know. And that's what happened with Ghost.

Instantly, I liked his vibe.

He had a nose ring. Painted black nails. Tall. Dark hair with a wave through it. Beautiful smile. Inked. Worked in the health industry. His profile wasn't detailed, but I liked his prompts. He seemed rather insightful and funny. The more I looked at him, the more I liked him.

So I pressed the little green heart and matched with him.

When I match with someone, I usually send them a message. I know, unheard of. To actually engage instead of matching and then never talking.

Seems weird, right?

But this is more common than actually conversing with people you've matched with—I don't get it, so don't ask me why.

I said hi.

He said hi back and asked how my day was.

Good grammar and punctuation. So he was already miles ahead of the rest.

Conversation with Ghost was easy from the get-go. His big energy had a positive vibe. He told me about his job. I liked that fitness was a big part of his life because it is in mine.

He asked what I did for work, and then we talked about our tattoos. He asked me something that caught my attention, and that was which of my ink was most meaningful. When I told him the anchor on my wrist as it's in honor of my father, he showed care and interest.

He shared that he always finds room to improve on something or look for something to strive for, as he loves ambition and dedication.

Everything he was throwing down, I liked.

Not one mention of a dick pic.

So I asked if he wanted to talk on a different platform as the dating apps gave me PTSD.

I sent him my handle, and he added me.

It was that simple and uneventful.

We spoke for a bit, but I didn't really feel anything other than interest in the beginning. There was something about him that I liked, though.

He was very positive, and he took the time to send messages that weren't one lines. He wrote paragraphs. And to a writer, someone who uses their words and not an emoji or a GIF as a response, well, that is akin to talking dirty.

We got to know one another briefly, and again, it wasn't anything remarkable. Just another guy I met who I found interesting.

That was until I sent him a picture, and he sent one back.

He was at work, and I don't know what it was, but seeing the person I had been talking to for a little while made me think, okay, so *now* you've got my attention.

He had that something, something.

His energy just shone.

His smile was big.

His hand tattoo extended to his wrist. Those were my favorite tattoos of all. The piece was so interesting. The longer you looked, the more you saw, and I guess that's what happened with Ghost.

He would send me regular messages during his break, which I liked. But I know from experience no one is more persistent than a man who wants to sleep with a woman. It's like their primal instinct is switched into overdrive, and the love bombing commences.

But I didn't think he was love bombing because his messages weren't filled with love or smut. They were genuine. And kind. And funny.

The event that turned things around was something I *do* remember.

It was a Friday night, and my Bunny, who I love with all my heart, asked me to go on an adventure with her. Of course I agreed.

This adventure took us to a land far, far away. When we arrived, I instantly got serial killer vibes. We waited and waited, but alas, another disappointment befell my bestie. She too has been a casualty to love, but she continues to believe in something that has done nothing but cause her pain.

She is the strongest person I know. She is my heart when mine stops beating.

During this time, Ghost sent me a text, and when I told him what we were doing, he said all I needed to do was say the word, and he'd come save us.

Not going to lie, I swooned just a little bit.

I have the Superman logo tattooed on me as a reminder that that's what I want in my man—for him to be my Superman, and I won't settle for anything less.

So when Ghost offered to be my Superman because I told him early on that was what I was looking for (and he looked like Henry Cavill, no word of a lie) I was hooked.

Ironically enough, like Bunny says, they always come back (think zombies wanting to eat your brains to replace theirs) and the same night, a guy I spoke to who had a girlfriend but failed to tell me when we were talking randomly messaged me. It went without saying that all contact ceased the moment I found out he had a girlfriend.

But he was back a few months later, like a dog in heat. He still had his girlfriend, but she was away. I don't need to draw a Venn diagram. You get the picture.

This deplorable but typical behavior of all cheaters made me appreciate Ghost all the more.

He texted me throughout the night, checking in on us to ensure we were safe. He offered to come meet us. He also offered to meet me at my house whenever I got home. He couldn't stay the night because he had work in the morning.

Before I could say I was not a booty call, he added that he wouldn't come in. He just wanted to meet me and give me a hug. But he also offered to meet somewhere halfway if I didn't feel comfortable giving him my address.

He just wanted to make sure I was okay.

And I believed him.

The shitty experience Bunny and I just underwent (apart from the hundreds of rabbits we saw in the field of dreams) made me appreciate Ghost so much because he cared.

He waited until I got home, messaging the entire time, and when I was safe, he bid me good night and said we would speak in the morning.

And he stuck to his word.

That simple gesture of kindness lured me in because, as sad as this is, kindness is a rarity today. So the fact that Ghost showed me something that should be expected behavior made him stand out from the rest.

From that day forward, I grew more attached.

We spoke so much.

Thousands of words bounced between us as we got to know one another, and to an author, that was our kryptonite.

He confided he was in a ten-year relationship and married for two of those years. That she didn't want to try new things, and he didn't want to miss out on all the beautiful things life had to offer.

I too confided in him about my marriage, and I guess our pain bonded us in a way.

He offered snippets of himself, and those pieces just drew me further in. He suffered from crippling depression, which he shared with me early on. He said he wasn't happy for a very, very long time, but I made him happy. That his energy was slowly becoming addicted to mine.

And I believed him because his messages spoke volumes.

The things he said to me were heartfelt and honest. They were filled with his fears and dreams. We spoke incessantly at night when both of us finished work. It was like message ping-pong—back and forth, back and forth.

There were no games.

No waiting a few minutes between messages because you didn't want to seem too eager.

I knew what Ghost wanted, and that was me.

He organized a date. I was impressed when he researched bars that served different mojitos—my favorite drink. Ghost took charge, something I liked in a man.

Another reason I liked Ghost was we didn't veer into the smutty talk until later. He was more interested in getting to know me than asking about sex.

I respected that.

But when we finally did, it just made me fall harder because I liked everything he said. The things he said to me were so hot. I was select in my tastes, but he was on the same page with everything I said I liked or wanted.

He drove me crazy.

He didn't ask for anything in return.

No naked pictures.

No late-night sexting.

No dirty phone calls.

Nothing.

We merely spoke about what we liked in the bedroom because we both agreed communication was the key to great sex.

Being attracted to someone physically was only a small part of what I looked for. I needed all the boxes ticked.

Intellect.

Heart.

Soul.

I needed all of these factors before I even contemplated going on a date.

Ghost had them all.

So if we vibed sexually, I knew I was in trouble.

And so did he.

He was an alpha in every sense of the word, but his kink was that he liked to please. He confessed to sleeping with quite a few girls, but said he, too, was fussy. He was all about people's energy, and if their energy didn't mix, then neither were they.

Even though we had now ventured into the forbidden land of sex talk, we never engaged in sexting. It was merely two adults discussing our likes and needs because it was apparent this was where our relationship was headed.

He messaged me every single morning from the day we met, wishing me a beautiful day.

I really loved that.

He was wedging his way into my world, and I found myself giddy the moment I saw his name light up on my phone, alerting me to a message. He was so thoughtful. Always asking how my day was and then went on to give me a rundown of his.

During this time, we sent one another maybe three or four photos, not many at all because our attraction wasn't based on looks, but we connected on an entirely different level. It wasn't shallow. We didn't fill our time with small talk.

What we spoke about was real.

I got hooked and hooked hard. This had never happened before so quickly. When I say I'm fussy, I mean it. I know there is no such thing as perfect, but Ghost was coming close to it.

He had a degree in literature. Wrote screenplays. Acted. Loved cinema and theater. And he was as big of a nerd as I was. We both were interested and involved in fitness and art. It was just another thing we had in common.

He wasn't afraid to share his life experiences with me—the good and the bad. I did the same.

I told him about the relationship I was in with Mr. J prior to him, hoping it would help him understand why I might grow distant at times. When I got too close, I ran. He said he did the same thing and promised to chase me if I ever ran.

He made it clear he didn't want me talking to anyone else as he was my "new guy." He was possessive and so damn dominant—I didn't stand a chance.

Ghost was so honest and expressive. He gave me so much. He would apologize if he didn't reply promptly. He never left me on read, something I really appreciated. He answered every question I asked and was sure to give me time.

He told me his friends had encouraged him to join the world of online dating to get out there and meet new people. But he confessed he didn't think it would take this long to get over his ex. I shared my experiences with him and said most times, we don't get over anything.

We just learned to deal with the pain.

His reply was him waving a big red flag. But I didn't see the warning signs because I didn't want to.

I try to be as expressive as I possibly can. I don't want people to think I'm dull or careless because it's the opposite. That was so beautifully written and so well said—holy shit. I was going to ask how does one move on, but I think you're right. One doesn't truly move on. Their lives just go on regardless of the memories and pain. I think the most important part is remembering why you left. You're so strong for doing it, and look at you now. You're absolutely killing life and making so much progress. I'm waiting for my turn to catch up. It's a long process, I know, but life's going to make me wait. I need to work for it more. I hope you have an amazing day full of love and happiness!

This message is an example of what Ghost would send. It's not a word-for-word account but a summary of the shit he would send.

To understand my story, you need to read the messages sent between us to see why I fell the way I did. This isn't love bombing in the traditional sense, this is someone opening up their heart to another human being.

He told me he couldn't stop thinking about me and had never wanted a girl more than he did me. He said the attraction he felt for me and how much he wanted me was something he never felt before. That our connection was on a whole different level.

I liked that because I felt the same way.

We were traveling full speed ahead when I probably should have slammed on the brakes. It felt right at the time, but perhaps it was too much, too soon?

Our date was a week away. But I grew impatient and wanted to see him earlier. I often wonder if this was my first mistake.

I spoke to my friends and asked their advice on inviting him over. It went against my whole not sleeping with a guy before the first date rule I have, but Ghost was different from anyone I had ever met before.

So perhaps a different set of rules should apply.

Which is why I asked him over after work.

Bunny was worried because inviting a stranger over to one's house before meeting them in public was an HBO special in the making. I told Ghost this, so he sent her a text message. It was so sweet and confirmed that I had made the right decision.

Hey Bunny, sending this for my girl. I promise to keep her safe.

Even Bunny swooned.

This was spontaneous, and although I do live my life this way, it's the total opposite when it comes to men. I like to plan and prepare.

I got ready, my heart in my throat the entire time.

Ghost went home after work to shower and get ready. He said he'd be at my house at 10 p.m.

At 9:58 p.m., there was a knock on my door.

I remember this moment so clearly because certain moments in your life are imprinted forevermore.

Meeting Ghost is one of those moments.

I opened the door, and when I saw him…I knew I was in so much fucking trouble.

The man I had been talking to incessantly was here, on my doorstep, and he was so much more in person. He smiled, and a dimple hit me in the solar plexus.

I was done for.

He didn't even say hello. He grabbed me by the throat and pushed me up against the wall, kissing the ever-living fuck out of me.

He stuck true to his word.

It was a move that every book boyfriend has done in your favorite story.

Once I believed he wasn't going to murder me in my sleep, I sent Bunny a text. Ghost smirked when I told him I was given strict orders to check in, and when I thanked him for messaging her, he said it was a request he never had before. But he liked it because it showed him that my friends cared.

My nerves soon appeared because now that the realization that he was real, and everything he said he was, I knew that my feelings were also real.

He was beyond gorgeous as his pictures did not do him justice. And I know he liked what he saw because the moment I put my phone away, he threw me onto the bed and showed me what a true alpha he really was.

We kissed unlike strangers, and that was because we had dissected one another prior to meeting.

I knew his secrets. And he knew mine.

So when the physical attraction was just as strong as the emotional, it resulted in the most explosive sex I'd ever had.

He kissed how I liked.

He smelled so good.

And he did things to me that I'm sure are illegal in at least ten different countries.

After all was said and done, he kissed my forehead, dragged me onto his broad chest, and said, "Come here and mold yourself to me."

He wanted the closeness. He wouldn't let me go.

After the things we did for hours, he still wanted that closeness because it wasn't enough.

I pressed my palm over his heart. "Your heart is beating so fast."

He smiled, and that was when I saw something that killed me—his teeth. They were so cute. I appreciate and see beauty in things that most don't notice, I guess.

He seemed caught off guard by my comment, but not in a bad way. Rather, he too could feel that our shared connection stemmed deeper than we both anticipated.

We spoke for hours after. Everything we spoke about through text, we now discussed face to face. It really was something else.

I think most would agree that sex with anyone for the first time is hit or miss. We're learning about the other person's body, their likes, and if the online connection can be felt physically. It's always different vibing with someone in person.

But with Ghost, it was even better than I thought it would be.

It was getting late, and he kissed me one final time. He peered down at me, those black nails of his caressing over my face.

"So our date…we're meeting at seven? Or eight?"

I was shocked he still wanted to go on our date, but he took my shock as rejection.

His brows drew inward, and a look of concern passed over his beautiful face.

"Yes? No? Yes?" he asked, hovering over me, worried I had changed my mind.

I didn't know why, but his insecurities touched me.

He was handsome, smart, and so clever. Yet here he was, my Superman, worried I would say no.

I replied the only way I could—I looped my fingers around the back of his neck, and toying with the strands curling his nape, I kissed him.

It was all the answer he needed.

It was late when he left. He kissed me good night in the doorway, and it was apparent it was hard for both of us to say goodbye.

When he left, I texted Bunny. Of course I told her everything. But then I grew sad. What if he didn't feel what I did? Men are different than women after sex. It's a scientific fact.

I began to panic and regret my choices.

But that was when my phone lit up because Ghost had sent a message.

I've made it home safely. I hope tonight made a good impression. Sorry, not sorry for making a mess.

My heart swelled because this message meant so much. Bunny was impressed. She said he's a keeper because a one-night stand does not text the moment they get home.

I replied.

Thanks for coming after working all day. You made more than a good impression. I can smell you all over me. Seeing you was supposed to help, not make things worse haha. I can't really read you, but I hope you felt what I did.

He replied a moment later.

I was more than happy to come over. You were so beautiful and intense. I hope my scent lingers for a while. I definitely felt something! You were everything you said you were. I shall speak to you tomorrow. Sleep well x

And this, dear reader, is why I fell so fucking hard because who wouldn't? Ghost was playing by a handbook crafted especially for me.

The following day, I woke sore all over—body and soul. The pain was a reminder that Ghost was, in fact, real. He felt like a dream. He did from the moment we kissed.

Ghost had sent a message before work. He wished me a beautiful day and said that he missed me. He then said something that any woman wanted to hear from her man.

I could barely get out of bed this morning.

I asked why.

Fucking you took it out of me.

I sent an eye emoji for him to elaborate.

'Cause my whole body melted the moment I came.

I didn't know what to think, so I asked if this wasn't the way he usually felt. His response:

I've never felt anything that I do with you before.

Well, fuck me, I was in trouble.

The entire day, I purposely didn't check my phone. I kept busy. I didn't want to miss a message from Ghost. I was trying not to be emotional, but the thought of this being a fling was hard to stomach.

I began questioning my decision. Was sleeping with him the wrong choice to make? Was he going to prove to be like most men out there?

But he wasn't.

He messaged me after work, just how he always did, asking how my day was and that he missed kissing me.

Where did this man come from? Was he too good to be true?

He was every book boyfriend come alive.

He was an alpha, but kind.

He was possessive over his girl and wasn't afraid to show it.

But most of all, he wasn't afraid to express himself in ways most women want and need from her man.

The night after we had sex was the night we spoke for hours. And that's no embellishment of the truth.

The sex had only brought us closer, and Ghost opened up to me so much so I honestly began to fall and fall hard.

This was fucking ridiculous, but I couldn't stop.

I told him he took my breath away, and his reply was:

I'm glad I take your breath away because you do the same. I'm just glad you liked me because you're so cute and gorgeous. And you do match me in the bedroom.

I was a goner…

He commended me on my career and how brave and confident I was putting my words on show for the world to pick apart. He admired my determination and called me strong, knowing how emotionally damaging being an author can be at times.

He just…got me.

We spoke about anything and everything. It was nonstop. It went on into the early hours of the morning. We were half asleep on the phone, not wanting to end our exchange. But in the end, sleep prevailed.

He made plans to see me on the weekend, and his sign-off was enough to leave me a giddy mess:

I can't promise I won't break you some more...

I was falling for Ghost, and not once did I ever question it.

It was a nice change as my previous "relationship" left me questioning who *I* was in the end. But not with Ghost.

He always told me I was beautiful. Or that he missed me. Without fail, he asked how my day was going. He was a sweetheart, a sweetheart with a filthy mouth because we just wanted another one more and more.

It was insane. Our chemistry left me breathless.

His passion left bruises, bruises which I asked for, and when I sent him a picture, his response, such an alpha:

I see I did some damage; consider it my way of marking you.

I couldn't wait to see him again.

The messages he sent were so fun and heartfelt and so damn HOT!

I like telling my girl what to do and ordering her around just before I put her in her place.
YES FUCKING PLEASE!

The morning of our date, however, Ghost texted me and did the unexpected:

Good morning, gorgeous. I'm sorry this is such a late reply! I've been absolutely flat out. I didn't catch a break yesterday. I'm okay. Just overwhelmed this week! We might need to push the mojitos. I'm sorry 🥺

I didn't know what to think. Had I been wrong about him this entire time? I refused to believe it, but this wasn't good.

My insecurities threatened to drag me under, and I was afraid I would surely drown this time. But Ghost knew me better than I thought when he sent a quick follow-up message.

And please don't overthink or get triggered. I'm here. Just busy, sadly. I miss you so much.

I had told him about my triggers and how I overthink. And he knew this would happen by postponing. But he put my mind at ease immediately.

He came back a few moments later, again to prove he wasn't canceling altogether.

Postpone till next Friday? All the drinks on me!

Okay, this was good. He was giving me an alternative date. He wasn't blowing me off, right?

The thing about an overthinker is that we are our own worst enemies. People tell us to calm down. Stop overthinking. Well, if we could, we would. But we can't. We want more than anything not to overthink, to trust and not make ourselves sick with worry, but it's not that easy.

Overthinkers need good communicators, and Ghost was just that. But this still got me feeling out of sorts. The harder we try to calm down, the worse things become.

And this was what happened.

The more I thought about it, the worse I felt. I don't need enemies. I don't need someone telling me I'm stupid or worthless and don't have a lick of talent because I tell myself this every single day. So when the boy I was falling for canceled our first proper date, these thoughts screamed so loudly that I had to cover my ears and shut out the noise.

But the noise was in my head. And it was getting louder and louder, so fucking loud that I couldn't breathe.

And when someone can't breathe, they panic. I thought he didn't like me. That I was making a fool out of myself. That he had lost interest and was too nice to say it.

And the message I sent reflected exactly that:

Have things cooled down? I felt like I knew what you wanted when we first started talking. I felt confident you wanted me as much as I wanted you. You were as hooked on me as I was on you. You were thinking about me all the time as I was with you. And you persisted to come see me every chance you got. Now, I don't really know. I LOVE that you're career-focused and ambitious. And that always comes first. But if you have no time for yourself, then how will you have time for me? And I would never expect you to. If I don't feel wanted, I will run away. I can't help it. Wish I could change it. I hope I haven't fucked anything up. I hope you still want to kiss. Sorry, am just thinking aloud.

This right here is inside the exasperating mind of an overthinker.

It doesn't make sense, but it does to me. I didn't see the fact he gave me reassurance and love. All I saw was him saying *no, I don't want to see you*. My scars are that deep and often prohibit me from seeing past the pain.

And when I am scared or in pain, I run.

I often get asked why I run for fun. And the answer is, the farther I run, the harder I push myself. I often feel as though I am running away from my trauma, and for a sliver in time, I can breathe. The voices quieten, and I feel at peace with my head and my heart.

So that's what I did.

I ran fifteen kilometers that day, and halfway through, Ghost replied.

I was so scared to see his response. I was certain he would run away like his predecessors. I wasn't worth the hassle.

I was high maintenance.

I was drama.

Or so I was told anyway.

But what I read…what I read was the moment I knew Ghost was different from any other man before him.

You haven't fucked anything up. Don't say that. You're literally the sweetest human being I've ever met. You're so caring, and I find it so beautiful you accept me for me. I don't want to stop kissing you. You kiss me so passionately, like I've always wanted to be kissed. This is how I am the majority of the time. I'll be upfront; I can get so caught up and can't manage work and my personal life. But I am trying to do what I can. I still want to try with you! I'm sending you big kisses, and yes, I still want to fuck the bejesus out of you.

That right there is a man who, regardless of his fears and anxieties, put me at ease. He was open and honest and assured me everything would be all right.

I needed to accept this for what it was, no matter how hard that was, and let nature take its course. I needed to trust in the universe because what you put out there is what you get back.

So I meditated.

I manifested.

I did anything to help clear my heart and mind.

Things eventually settled, and then, three days later, we had our date.

I was so nervous.

I consulted with Mötley on what to wear.

We decided cute but casual.

I wore a black little romper, showing off my leg tattoos which I know he liked. My makeup was simple, but my signature red lips were the star of the show.

Ghost knocked on my front door.

I opened it and saw he had red roses in his hand. He had on black jeans and a black shirt, which complemented his three-day growth.

He offered me the flowers and kissed my cheek.

He smelled so damn good.

Once the roses were in water, he drove us to a vegan restaurant. He had told me he was organizing it all. I was beyond impressed. He tried everything I suggested, regardless of the fact that he wasn't vegan. I don't force my beliefs on anyone, but it touched me he would try something new, knowing how important being a vegan is to me.

Ghost wasn't afraid of PDA. He held my hand. He kissed me briefly as he got up to use the restroom. And he made sure everyone knew I was there with him.

This was such foreign ground for me, but I soon learned the rules, and I liked everything he was throwing down.

When we left, he held my hand and kissed me under an arch of lights. It was the perfect first date. He took me home, but I was surprised when he didn't come inside.

He had to work early, and I respected that. His work ethic was admirable. I also liked that this, whatever it was, wasn't based on sex.

He did yank me onto his lap and kiss the ever-living fuck out of me before I went inside, unable to wipe the smile clean from my face.

Ghost came over during the week.

The message he sent a day before made me giddy:

You're so beautiful. I miss your lips so much. I just want to make out and kiss you so passionately all over. One more sleep and I'm all yours, and well, one more sleep and I'll be destroying you all over…

And he kept true to his word.

The moment I opened the door, I saw him and nothing—*nothing*—existed but him.

He pulled me into his arms and kissed me like it was the last thing he was doing before he died.

He smashed me up against the wall and kissed me with passion and love—my most favorite kiss of all. He was vocal, and I loved that he didn't mask the effect I had on him. It reminded me of the text he sent that said I kissed him how he always wanted to be kissed.

I pulled his hair.

He grabbed my throat.

He bit me all over.

My god…the things we did that night.

The sex lasted for a very long time. It was intense. It was the stuff you read about in the books I write. But I was living out every scene I had ever written with the one MC who was stealing my heart and soul.

He was rough.

He was soft.

He kissed me until my lips were swollen.

He fucked me so hard, I cried.

He threw me around and owned me because that night, I was his, and he was mine. I didn't think I'd ever felt more connected to another human being than I did that night.

It was far more than sex.

It was a tether between two broken souls who stayed afloat by the other.

I fell head over heels for Ghost that night.

It just wasn't the sex. Okay, maybe it was a little the sex. But the way he touched me, the way he made sure I was all right when he defiled me over and over again, it was fucking raw and still kills me to this day.

He looked into my eyes and pressed his forehead to mine as we locked as one.

He never broke eye contact.

He wasn't gentle, but he was.

I know that doesn't make sense, but he consumed me. And I allowed it because I lowered my walls for the first time ever and let him in.

It was take and give.

Give and take.

We were lost in one another, and it was so much more than I ever thought it would be.

He dragged me onto him, and I pressed my ear to his chest, listening to the steady staccato of my lover's heart—a heart that was so big, too big for this world.

We spoke for a long time. About anything and everything. He caressed my back. I ran my fingers through his hair.

It was everything I wanted. *He* was everything I wanted.

We interlaced hands, and I loved looking at his black fingernails.

His hands healed me in every single way.

We had spoken over the past few days about his birthday, which was tomorrow. He said he never celebrated it, so I wanted to make it special this year.

I hinted I wanted to get a gift, but he objected to that strongly. He said what we did the night we first met was gift enough.

He never asked me for anything, so I got him something small, but it meant the world.

Superman is an important part of my life, since I was a child, as he reminds me of my dad. So because Ghost was soon becoming my Superman, I got him something to represent that.

It was small—a Superman key chain with a little blackboard for a card which read:

You're my Superman.

Happy Birthday x

He opened it and instantly put the key chain on his keys. It meant so much to us both.

I also gave him a cupcake with a candle and sang him "Happy Birthday." He was touched, like it was something no one had ever done for him before.

He ate the cupcake, then kissed me with frosting all over his mouth.

Those were happier times.

We kissed that night at my door, unable to say goodbye. He said he would organize another date at the zoo or aquarium this time, as he knew I loved animals.

We made such big plans.

He slapped my ass as he always did, and then he left.

But those plans never came to fruition because that kiss, that intense kiss, was to be our last…I just didn't know it yet.

Love ♡ HardER

Good night, beautiful. I hope you have an amazing sleep full of beautiful dreams. I miss you so much, you sexy fucking goddess. I shall speak to you in the morning.

That was what I woke to.

I had fallen asleep and didn't receive his message until the morning and only awoke to another message he sent early in the day.

Thank you for my gift. I really love it, and I will cherish it. Now, I feel like Henry Cavill more than ever. I hope you had an amazing sleep and don't feel too crippled. I'm sorry I'm hard to read. I don't try to be. You're way too beautiful.

I had messaged him before I went to sleep that he was hard to read, which he was. My overthinking brain began to tick over the moment he left. I wish it would stop. But something so perfect can't be real. History has proven this.

You're so welcome. Hope you have a beautiful birthday ♥ I may be a little crippled, but well worth it 🐼 and please don't be sorry! I guess it's always different seeing someone in person as opposed to messaging and if those feelings reflect into real life. It's always different for me. Wanted to know how you feel, I guess?

I didn't hear from him until after work. It touched me that he always messaged the moment he finished.

My day has been really great, not as depressing as I thought it would be. I'm sorry you're sore haha, but I definitely did warn you it'd be like that. I feel okay, sweetness, like you're beautiful and have one of the purest souls I've ever encountered. If I seem distant, it's only because I haven't really been with anyone else, and I think the fact that I'm still in the process of healing from my past means I can become stuck in my head a bit. Like you're perfect in every way, I am just adjusting to the fact I'm not with that said person.

Thank you for being honest. You're so emotive and expressive. It's beautiful to read. You're not distant. Just hard to read, I guess. But that's so okay 🙏 I too get in my head, and I like you…a lot, and I'm scared. We're both healing, it seems, but I want you to know I would never hurt you. I will always respect your decisions. I just ask, if you're comfortable doing so, that you tell me what you're thinking 'cause I overthink, and for the past two years, I've been mentally destroyed. So I don't want to assume anything. Prefer to ask you if I'm curious. And vice versa. And on a side note, I never want any pressure. Things are easy between us. And I really love that. That's why I overthink because you are everything that I want. And in regard to healing, sometimes we just learn to deal with the loss and start over, I guess, but never really get over it. But we learn from it and appreciate it for what it was and grow from it. That's how I see things with my past because it's the past, and that's where I want it to remain. Although it still hurts sometimes, I remember why I left and who I am now, and how much happier I am. Then the pain lessens, and I appreciate who I am now and how that person is happier because of those life lessons. You have to experience the darkness to appreciate the light, and you and your cute teeth are my light x

I think it's important to be expressive, though I have a hard time doing it, especially when it's in my head, like I can be bubbly and full of laughter or completely quiet and in deep thought the next moment. I spend a lot of time running through scenarios. I didn't think it'd take me this long to try to heal from it, and yes, like you, I am scared too. My relationship was a third of my life, and sometimes it hurts that I do not have that relationship with that person. I'm still accepting things.

Our texts grew so intense, and it soon became our norm. This was how we conversed, and I loved it. But I worried all the talk of the past might taint what we have.

I've been thinking about the above, and I don't want our pasts to taint anything between us. How about we focus on the future and not the past? Let's make happy, fun memories together involving cute animals and you slapping my butt?

He of course put my mind at ease with his beautiful words and heart.

Your words really do touch my soul, and I definitely needed to hear it. I always try to

focus on the future and strive toward something. Regardless of the weight of my past. We are both victims of troubled relationships, and I envy your outlook on life. It's so beautiful and motivational. I can only hope mine is as strong-willed as yours. I am trying, though! Nothing but the future...no past, just present day and what comes beyond. Cute animals? Butt slapping? Darling, you already got me intertwined.

I was blinded by his words, but the signs were there—I just didn't want to see them. I wanted to believe he would heal and we could do that together. But the cracks were starting to show.

I was Ghost's first relationship after his marriage ended. This wouldn't end well.

Yet I stuck in there because I wanted him. I meant every word I said to him.

One night, I asked him a simple question: *What's the catch?* Because he was too good to be true.

That just might be my objective here—to put you in your place. Young guy destroys successful book author. I like that a lot. Hahaha, there's no catch. I'm just trying to find my person, and you, miss, are ticking quite a lot of boxes. You're gorgeous, small, ambitious, confident, and funny. I love all those qualities. I like the energy you give off. Mine is slowly feeding on it. It's getting its taste.

I didn't know what to say. Ghost left me speechless. But I tried to express how I felt.

For an author, I really suck when trying to find the right words to reply to you at times. You leave me breathless in every single way. And you've thrown me on my ass—both literally and figuratively 😂 I wasn't looking for you, but here you are, making me think about you more than I should. You're incredibly special, and I am so hooked on you 🥺 Yes, you're an amazing kisser and so damn hot, but that is a small part of what I look for. It's all the other things I am hooked on which kill me. I'm not sure what it all means...as I'm not sure what you're looking for in terms of what you're looking for in me. But I never want any pressure between us. Ever x Have an amazing night. Be safe. And only if you wanted, please slap any girl who touches you from me 😍😂 I miss

you. I miss your mouth xx

And his reply, his reply was by far the most heartfelt anyone, ANYONE had ever sent me.

You're so beautiful and kind...I love the way you talk to me. It's so mature and sexy. I feel glad that I can leave you speechless. I literally just try to be myself always. Be hooked on me because I'm hooked on you. I want to fuck you into submission and cuddle you back to health. I'm not sure what it all means either, but we've clearly met each other for a reason. Only time can tell us. But what I do know is that I'm insane about you. I can't stop thinking about you either, and I want nothing more than to just be inside you, looking deep into your eyes.

I needed to include these so you can see what I was dealing with and why I fell so hard for him.

I know some have said he love bombed me. Or that he was a narcissist, and perhaps he was. But these words touched me so profoundly at the time, and I believed every single word.

These excerpts were merely a drop in the ocean of the messages we exchanged. He wrote paragraphs filled with his feelings and emotions; you couldn't fake that. Well, at least I liked to believe he didn't.

Ghost was becoming my heart, and all I wanted was to be his.

The inevitable has arrived.

We all knew it was coming.

I still don't understand it, but you've stuck with me, so you deserve to know how it all ended.

It happened over a week or so. I really can't remember. But there was a shift. Slight at first, but it was there.

Reading back over his messages, I see him retreating. It breaks me to read them because I can't help but wonder what I could have done differently.

What's between us is so raw and so beautifully innate. Having this kind of connection is so rare, and I don't want to let that go unexplored. I accept you for you because I want you—the good. The bad. All of it. You've said you want to protect me. Well, I want to protect you too. Let me be your strength on the days when yours may be lost. I will never stand in the way of your dreams and career. I will always support you because I want you to be happy. I'm sorry I get in my head. It's something I'm trying to work on. I sometimes need reassurance. Thank you for not running away. If I run away, please chase me. You really are my Superman ❤

You're so beautiful and sweet. Not to mention sexy and hot. Like you can really fuel a fire in me that burns, and I just want to explode. Your words mean so much to me. I love that you are willing to accept all of me, the baggage weighing me down, my work ethic, my ambition. That means more than you'll ever know. Sometimes one just longs to be understood and accepted. You can be absolutely everything, and I'll be the same for you.

Although his messages were still heartfelt, I went from receiving endless messages from Ghost to maybe one or two a day.

I wanted to believe he was busy with work, but something was happening in the background—I just didn't know what.

Months since we first started talking, he didn't text me all day, which wasn't like him at all as he'd made an effort to message me every day since we first connected.

I sent a photo of myself blowing a kiss with the caption: *Just wanted to make sure you're okay?*

Good morning! First things first, you're so stunning I can't fathom it. I hope you slept well. I'm okay. I had a bad day yesterday as I had to fire two people, and it just carried on outside of work too. It really depleted me and put me in a bad mood. Work life to personal life balance is way off atm. Only because I'm juggling a little too much than I can handle, I think. I'm not sure when I'll see you next. I need to get some replacements ASAP.

My heart and brain went into overdrive, but I needed to calm the fuck down. This was Ghost. The man who'd stuck with me for months. No way was he having a change of heart.

Hell to the fuck no!

Oh, that sucks. I'm so sorry & I can only imagine how hard that was. Are you okay? Life is about balance. Do what you can and remember your well-being; your happiness comes first. You can't help others if you're burned out. I meant what I said—I'm here for the good and the bad. I know you're not always going to be happy. But neither am I. I'm here to hug you and listen to you. I'm a really good listener. I'd rather that than not talking or seeing you at all. I miss you. I miss your mouth. I also miss your smile when you look down at me in bed 'cause those teeth. Do you realize you do that? Sending so many kisses x

I needed him to see his worth as I could sense his depression was creeping in, and he shared that when that happens, he retreats.

You're so sweet and beautiful. That's such a beautiful message and so reassuring. You're wayyyy too kind for this world. It certainly doesn't deserve you. Thank you for saying my happiness matters. It's something I definitely struggle with a lot. I miss you too, gorgeous. Miss absolutely everything about you. Miss the way you kiss me. You actually think my teeth are cute? They're always something I've been self-conscious of, but I'm learning to love them because of you. Thank you for sending me kisses. I'm sending twice as many back and many, many dirty thoughts to you.

Things seemed okay, right?

But they weren't.

These are the last messages ever exchanged between Ghost and me. Should I have known they were, I would have said so much more.

Why do you struggle with your happiness? Well, we're going to change that. What's one thing that makes you happy? I don't care how trivial it is. We're going to do that together. Think on it and tell me and let's do it ♥ *And your teeth are FUCKING ADORABLE!*

I haven't been a happy guy in a long, long time. I just find it hard to find joy in things. It

Love♡HardER

possibly has to do with being underserving. I think about how lucky some people are to have everything handed to them, yet I work, work, work, but I'm only getting so far. I know it's stupid because I should be grateful I'm alive, which I am. I just wish there wasn't so much struggle. I hope you're having the best day ever. You truly deserve it, you sexy fucking minx.

This was the first time he expressed his unhappiness with his life. I thought he was happier than he was, but I was wrong. The signs were there. I just didn't want to accept them.

It's not stupid at all. Your feelings are never stupid. Don't disregard your successes. Look at what you've achieved instead of what you haven't. You've got goals and aspirations, and all good things take time. I hate that you're not happy. It makes my heart sad 'cause I wanna change that ♥ What can I do? You say you find it hard to find joy in things...how about we try something totally different? What's something that'll make you happy? I'm going to brainstorm ideas all day now... I'm going overseas for work soon. Wanna come? X

I really fucking tried. I've not read over these messages since they were sent. But if it helps me, if it perhaps helps *you* heal, then here we go…the final message Ghost ever sent to me. Read it and decide if I was wrong in being totally confused why he disappeared off the face of the earth after sending me this…

Gosh, you're so amazing…I really fucking love this…you make me feel like I'm not stupid and make me have hope for myself. By being yourself, you make me happy. I love people who just be true to themselves. Because I try to be true to myself. Next week, yes, I'm coming over to do some more damage to you 🌀 Your words actually floor me. I hope you know that…like honestly! I'm trying to be the person the world needs. I'm glad I can keep you on your toes, you sexy fucking minx. It's not me if I don't make you tiptoe just a little bit. The only place I want to travel with you is in your soul. I want us to merge and travel the universe in our eyes.

The end…

What a cliffhanger, right?

But this is real life. This is the ending I was given and expected to fill in the blanks.

After that message, I wasn't expecting to be ghosted, but I was.

But this isn't how my story ends…

I sent this in response:

You kill me. You fucking kill me. That last paragraph, tho… Can you get any hotter? Fml 😊 You're working toward something. Don't ever forget that. Things may be hard, but you're focused on what you want. You're so driven. Good things will come. Don't let your past or insecurities taint it. You're paving the path for your future, and I'm here to hold your hand ♥ I want you to stop and think about all your accomplishments. Think of everything you've been through and how you've never given up. You want more. And you're fighting for more. That's fucking incredible. So don't ever sell yourself short. I'm here to cheer you on and always support you because I think you're beyond amazing. You do more than keep me on my toes. You kill me in every single way. Mind. Body. Soul. I'm so excited to see you next week. Lame, right? 😂

I've not read this message until now because I was too scared to. I thought I had said the wrong thing because Ghost opened this message and did what he NEVER did…he left me on read.

I didn't understand, so I sent another message the day after.

You usually always reply. Have I said too much? Are you okay? x

Nothing.

Nada.

My friends assured me it would be okay. That perhaps the pressures from work were too much, and he needed time, so I left it. I did everything I could to distract myself, but the silence was so deafening that I couldn't think.

I sent him a video saying I hoped he was okay.

He never opened it.

I sent him another message a couple of days later.

Beautiful boy, I'm worried about you. If you don't wanna talk anymore, or your feelings have changed, then I accept that and will leave you be. I never want any pressure between us, but please don't go silent on me. This doesn't seem like you. Are you okay?

Crickets…

By this stage, I was experiencing all the stages of loss. Grief. Anger. Confusion. I was hooked on the most potent drug—love—and it was ripped away from me, and now, now I was jonesing. I was desperate for my next fix because my heart and pride couldn't stand being ignored.

So I sent another message.

I'm here, and not going anywhere unless you want me to. I hope you're okay. I miss you x

Nothing…

Over a week had passed and Ghost was just that. My heart was broken. But I couldn't give up.

Hi. Here's your daily reminder that you're incredible and that I want to hug and kiss you. I'm here, and I still stand by everything I've said to you. I hope you're okay. I miss you x

I may as well have screamed into an abyss because my texts were delivered but never read.

I don't know how many tears I cried over him. I just know the pain is just as raw. I was worried he had done something awful, that perhaps his depression had conquered him in the worst possible way.

But now, I see that Ghost was a selfish motherfucker who could have answered ANY of these messages. But he chose to ignore me. And now that I can see that, I'm angry at myself for chasing him when he didn't deserve a second thought.

Bunny also reached out because she was worried. She too was ignored.

This was bad. So bad that the hole in my chest grew every single day. Ghost leaving ripped open a wound far bigger than the one he helped heal because I was angry with myself for letting him in.

How could I have been so stupid?

There was no activity on his socials, and I was worried. I thought perhaps he was in his cave recharging his batteries just as he said he did at times, so I waited…for weeks.

Those weeks, I ran the most I've ever run in my entire life. It was all I could do to make myself feel remotely better. The more pain I was in, the better I felt. The pain made me feel something other than being numb. It felt as though I was running away from my problems, but no matter how far I ran, they always caught up to me.

I was broken once again, but this time, I didn't think I would heal. And truth be told, I still haven't healed.

I often wonder when this sadness will go away. It only seems to grow. Each time I open my heart up and love, I leave a piece of myself with the one who breaks me. Now, I feel like I'll never heal. I'm just learning to live with all these missing pieces because I refuse to give up.

I'm too stubborn to.

I don't know why I keep going back to love. As a child, we learn not to touch something hot or it'll burn. Why, as an adult, do we keep going back to the one thing that burns us over and over again?

No matter how many times I tell myself this is the last time, I find myself in the same predicament, clearly a glutton for punishment. I suppose the high I get from being "in love" is the reason I don't learn. Or maybe I'm just a hopeless romantic wishing to believe it's different this time.

Love has given, but it's also taken so much.

Love♡HardER

When will it stop? When will I find that person who will love me as much as I love them? I have love to give...but no one to give it to.

Then something happened...he viewed a story.

When I saw his name, I had to sit down. That was how badly he affected me. He didn't make contact, but he was alive. That's all I cared about.

There was silence for another week.

I didn't reach out. I couldn't. I needed to give him time because I didn't know what he experienced. So again, I waited...the most impatient person waiting for the man she wanted to come back to her and explain what went wrong.

What a fucking fool I was.

A week later, he viewed another story.

The same thing happened the next day.

And the day after that.

Yet no contact. He was watching me from afar. Tormenting me with his fucking screen name. I was a mess. I couldn't write. I couldn't think. I simply waited for Ghost to return.

But he never did.

He chose to be a fucking coward instead when he unfollowed me on my socials and removed me as a friend.

I am not a social media fan, but this one, this stung.

What did I do?

All I did was show him love, and in return, he ignored me for weeks, then spied on me, only to unfollow me.

I was hurt.

I cried.

But most of all...I was fucking pissed.

So with my head held high, I sent him one final message.

You promised you're not the type of guy who sleeps with a girl and then leaves. You promised you'd treat me right 'cause you saw the way your dad treated your mom. You said you'd be my Superman. I am who I said I was. And I thought you were real. But I don't know what happened between us. Regardless, I hope you find happiness. You deserve it x

I didn't feel a thing. I was utterly numb.

A day later, he blocked me. But I didn't care because, guess what, you can block someone in real life—it's called boundaries.

I didn't know what to do.

I mourned, I guess.

I spoke to Bunny, Angel, and Mötley—my ride or dies who never once told me to shut up. They listened to me for HOURS upon HOURS. They never said I was better off. Or that I needed to move on. They let me talk and listened because that's what friends do.

I was lost, and well, I did some reckless things.

I am all for living in the moment, so I don't regret a thing. But when hurt, I hide. I don't deal with my emotions because who the fuck wants to deal with those. I built a fortress around myself and watched my kingdom burn to the ground by my own hand.

It was ugly, but I just wanted to feel something other than pain. I wanted to fill the void he left behind, but nothing helped.

I wanted to send him so many texts. It took all my willpower not to go to his work because that would not have achieved anything.

Ghost made his choice, and that choice wasn't me.

Like Bunny said, unless he lost his vision and his fingers got severed, there's no excuse for him not to text or call. He chose that option. He chose to ignore me when he knew it would hurt me.

But he didn't care.

I wish *I* didn't, but I did.

I looked for him in other men, but no one could compare. I was broken, so damn broken, I didn't know how to be unbroken.

I hated it.

I was taught to be strong.

I was raised to never quit.

But so many days, I wanted to give up.

All love did was hurt me. But I guess I hurt myself by choosing the men that I do.

But Ghost was different, wasn't he?

You've read his messages. Would you have seen through his lies?

But I couldn't believe he was lying. It couldn't have not been real. Of course, he felt everything he said he did, right?

Wrong…

His actions proved who he was. He was a coward. He would rather hide in the shadows than live in the light because he was scared.

I was faced with endless possibilities, and this is why ghosting is a horrible thing to do to another human being in the dating world.

Being a ghostee, I can highly say I do not recommend.

I felt like a ghost; barely here nor there. Perhaps the term coined for such an event is an appropriate one after all.

I invested so much time and energy into someone who thought it was okay to stop talking just because. He wasn't worth it, I knew that, but I couldn't stop thinking about him. The more I tried, the angrier and sadder I became.

My emotions were like a yo-yo because I literally could change in a breath. Or feel both at the same time. I was fighting with myself, with my mind. I felt like I was going insane. To take that power away from someone is cruel. Not to mention, that's just weak.

But I didn't want to believe he wasn't who he said he was because, what did that say about me? I needed to forget him, but I couldn't.

He haunted my waking hours, and when I tried to sleep, he became my nightmare. I couldn't escape him. I was helpless to my mind, which wouldn't rest until I was driven insane.

I sank to my lowest point and fell into a darkness which I never thought I'd ever pull myself from. Those were scary times.

But then, something happened, something which I like to believe was the universe talking to me…and making sure I listened this time.

I wasn't looking, but he found me.

And his name—his name was Switzerland.

I knew I couldn't keep him, but he stayed with me for as long as he could.

He too was guarded because he was leaving me in nine weeks to live in another country—forever.

Like forever, forever.

This was another heartbreak in the works, but I don't do easy. But the thing with Switzerland is that he was. If he wasn't leaving, I would have kept him as my always because he was kind but bossy, talented, determined, strong, and HOT. And unlike any man I have ever been with before, he was real.

Writing about him is bittersweet because I always wonder what could have eventuated between us. But he was the sensible one, the one who drew the line and said we should limit how much we saw one another to save ourselves the heartache when he left.

He was right, but it didn't mean it didn't suck.

So, I lowered my walls and opened my heart, and although broken, I let Switzerland in. And you know what happened?

I was happy for a little while.

Even though our time always came with an expiration date, I made the most of this unique connection with an extraordinary man who caught me off guard. I had bursts of happiness when I was with Switzerland. He made things…normal.

And I felt safe in his arms.

Ghost was becoming a distant memory, right?

Well, almost, but you didn't think this would end in a happily ever after, did you?

There was no way Ghost was getting away with ghosting me. The longer I thought about it, the more unsettled I grew. And that grew and grew. It festered and festered like a cystic pimple until one day…

PLOT TWIST.

Ghost wasn't a ghost anymore…

✈ SWITZERLAND ✈

SWITZERLAND

Switzerland came out of nowhere, which is ironic, considering the impact he was about to make.

I didn't tell anyone about him at first because I didn't even know what to say. But it was only three days of talking before we met. There was something about Switzerland I liked.

Perhaps it was because he made it clear early on that he didn't play games. He went after what he wanted, and it was apparent he was a complete alpha.

I also didn't want to waste time because he was leaving. So when he asked for my number, I gave it to him without wondering if I would wake up in a bathtub of ice with a missing kidney.

I remember one of the first things he said when he called me. "Hi, I'm Switzerland. I'm your new boyfriend."

And it just stuck.

I called him my boyfriend, and he called me his girl.

We were two human beings who gravitated to one another. It didn't feel as though we had met as strangers. It felt as though we had known one another forever.

I went to his house, and he showed me his setup. Switzerland was a very talented DJ. He was moving to better his career since he had accomplished everything he could here.

I admired his decision and found him to be so brave.

We spoke for a very long time until Switzerland told me we were going into his bedroom. He wasn't presumptuous or crass; he was bossy, but in that sexy alpha sort of way that I like.

I followed, not really sure what to expect. The first time with someone is always an exciting but scary experience. Will they live up to the hype in your head? Or will they be a huge disappointment, leaving you wishing you'd stayed home instead?

However, the moment he hugged me, everything became still and safe. He appeased my heart and mind, but because of Ghost, I had my walls firmly affixed into place.

But it was hard not to soften when Switzerland cuddled me and kissed my neck. There was perhaps apprehension to his touch. I liked that.

He was tender but wild.

Bossy but kind.

Being with him was different from Ghost, so I surrendered. From the first moment we kissed, I knew he was about to change my world.

I didn't know how or why. I just knew he made the pain go away.

He didn't smother me.

He didn't expect anything from me.

He just wanted to be with me. And I felt the same way about him.

We spent hours with one another. We lay together, and he told me a story in German. It was by far the cutest first date I ever had.

I liked the way he spoke. He was articulate and clever. I liked the way he smelled. Being with him felt natural. You just know when someone is your person, and Switzerland was mine.

He was tall, inked, and had the most beautiful face I had ever seen. He was incredibly expressive, something I don't think he is aware of. His smile made me smile.

I love hand tattoos, and Switzerland's were incredible. A tiger on one hand and a clock on the other.

The thing about Switzerland is that he was so incredibly humble. I didn't realize how talented he was until I asked a friend who fanboyed when I told him we had kissed. He gave me the lowdown on who he was in the music world, and I suddenly liked him all the more because he never hinted at his success. I didn't like him for his successes, however. Admired? Yes. But I liked him more because of how humble he was.

We had a second date a week later.

It was even cuter than the first.

Switzerland always made lots of eye contact with me. When engaging in conversation, he always held my attention.

There is something about a man who can hold his own.

The more time I spent with Switzerland, the more things I saw and liked. Honestly, there wasn't one thing that I didn't like.

He was so kind to me.

I felt comfort and affection in his presence, and when we lay together, I was at peace. The simple things with him provided me with a warmth I hadn't felt with anyone else in a long time.

His heart was so big.

He wasn't motivated by sex. He was the total opposite. Being the smutty romance author, I felt like I was corrupting him half the time. But it was a totally different story when we were in the bedroom.

He was a fucking beast.

The things he used to say to me? Oh my lord, I can't even think about them without dying a little inside. They weren't dirty talk. They were the total opposite.

He was so hot, and he didn't even realize how much so, which just made him all the more hotter.

It was hard giving in to him, but with time came trust, and when Switzerland proved his loyalty by always sticking to his word, I let him in.

But Switzerland had his own walls firmly in place.

In this world, I've learned that every person does.

Most times, those walls are there because of love and love hurting them. But he still allowed me in a little—he crossed the moat to meet me but always retreated into his castle so I could never get too close.

His past shaped him into the man he was, and that man was so exceptional.

But I always felt that Switzerland held me at arm's distance.

He never wanted me to get too close, which frustrated me. I wanted to know him, and although he shared so much, I felt he was perhaps wrestling with his head and his heart.

There was always a distance between us, and I hated the divide.

I know he was trying for us not to get attached, but my mindset was different from his. I wished for us to make as many memories as we could so when he left, we would have nothing but happy times to look back on.

He didn't agree.

He was bossy and so damn stubborn, so I was never able to change his mind. I wish that I had because I always felt like we were both holding back. It's the one regret I have. Not to know what could have been.

Perhaps deep down, I knew he was right. But his leaving was going to suck regardless if we spent one day a week together or every day.

But I didn't press because I was too broken to. I didn't want to deal with another rejection.

Although Switzerland helped me heal, my feelings for Ghost forever simmered in the background. I knew that wouldn't be the case if Switzerland let me in. I felt I was getting pieces of him, but not enough to show me who he really was.

The pieces he did share with me, I liked a lot.

Love ♡ HardER

But how can you fall in love with half a person?

You can't.

Switzerland was holding back, and although I understood it, it was hard to give him all of me for that exact reason.

We were exclusive during our time together because I didn't want anyone other than him. He was the one who laid down the "rules," but I liked that he felt content with what we shared.

We went on cute dates. We hung out in my room watching TV. We kissed. We laughed—we laughed, a lot. He bought me roses just because. And we had a lot of mind-blowing sex. We did all the things a normal couple does, but we weren't normal or a couple because the inevitable always lingered.

He was leaving, and I would be left to deal with the aftermath.

The person left behind is reminded of the memories made, while the person who leaves is ready to make new memories in a new place and with someone else.

This was constantly playing over and over in my mind—the mind of the overthinker, remember? I wanted to pretend his leaving wouldn't hurt, but I knew it would.

So I distanced myself as best I could.

I never sought out the comfort of other men because I didn't want anyone else, but I distracted myself with work and friends.

But the sadness returned. Or I guess it never left.

It just lessened when I was with Switzerland.

I saw Switzerland every week from the first moment we met until the day he left. He will always be my biggest regret in life because I will never know what we could have been.

But deep down, I know that we could have been exceptional.

I wanted to explain who Switzerland is because a month before he was leaving, it was as if the universe sensed I was slowly relearning how to trust again because it threw me a motherfucking curveball that destroyed me once more.

Switzerland slowly retreated. Day by day, the messages became less frequent, and the time between each response seemed to get longer and longer. I was watching him leave me in slow motion, and there wasn't a thing I could do about it.

When we saw one another, it was good. So good, in fact, but when he was gone, it was as if I imagined the whole thing because he just wouldn't exist in my world.

It was hard to accept because when together, he would say things that made me think he was just as attached as I was becoming. But when I say he is stubborn, I mean he is the MOST stubborn man I have ever met.

He knew what he wanted, and that was to further his career in another country far, far away.

He never made a secret of the fact. But I guess I hoped he would recognize the connection we shared as something worth making a sacrifice for.

But it seemed those walls he had erected around himself were higher than I thought.

He still sent me polite messages because that's the type of man Switzerland was. He would never ghost, but he ensured I knew this wasn't a serious thing for him. He would get on that plane in a month and never look back.

I wish I was stronger to end things then and there or not start anything in the first place, but my history has proven I don't make the smartest choices when it comes to men.

Switzerland's distance began to hurt, and the feelings of emptiness grew once more. Like I said, they never went away but merely dimmed when I was with Switzerland. He never told me what was wrong, only that he has walls behind walls to protect himself.

Those walls were lowered when we kissed. Or when we lay in silence, in one another's arms. But as D-Day approached, I felt as though his walls were reerected and reinforced.

I didn't stand a chance.

Switzerland was always a battle I was destined to lose.

I was tired, so tired of fighting. How much can a person take before they just switch off and become numb to it all?

I was trying my best to accept Switzerland's departure, but it hurt a lot. I tried not to get attached, but I clearly am a romantic at heart. Switzerland, however, he was just moving forward with his life, and it was apparent that I was no longer his girl.

I was trying to focus on anything other than my heart being broken—again, when an author friend of mine gave me a call.

He had a proposition for me.

He was writing a book and wanted me to be on the cover.

I was honored and totally flattered.

He went into detail that he had found the perfect male lead to pose alongside me. He asked him, and the guy semi-agreed. However, he was self-conscious and doubted he was book cover material, but Zuko saw potential in him.

I asked what he looked like, and I should have known that the universe wasn't done with me. Lesson number…I've lost count: when the universe talks to you, listen.

My friend, Zuko, detailed a gorgeous man he had seen working at a fitness center—the same place where Ghost worked. He had dark hair with some gray throughout. A scar in his left eyebrow. He was tall, muscled, and smelled like heaven.

My heart began to race.

I asked what else.

He went into detail that he had a tattoo on his hand which extended up his wrist. Oh, and a nose ring. And in case there was any confusion, his name was Ghost.

I didn't know if this was a good or bad thing. I mean, this was my chance to get the answers I had desperately sought for months.

But did I really want to go back there?

I was in no way healed from what happened with Ghost, but I couldn't deny this as a sign from the heavens. I'm a big believer in signs. There are no such things as coincidences, and this right here was a sign that it was time to take back what was stolen from me.

Zuko said he may have accidentally on purpose showed Ghost a photo of me.

I frantically asked what Ghost did when he saw my photo, and Zuko said he stared at the picture for a good twenty seconds before saying he would think about the shoot.

And that was it.

As anticlimactic as it is, Zuko said there was no recognition on Ghost's face.

Zuko picked up on my panic, and I told him that I thought I knew who Ghost was. I briefly told him our history and asked if he was sure Ghost didn't recognize me.

He said he simply looked at the photo for a very long time.

Had he forgotten me already? Was I that insignificant to him that he had forgotten I existed?

There was no way I could let this go because this was the opportunity every ghostee wishes for—to get answers and ask the profound question:

Why?

Most women would let it go and move on, but I couldn't. This was a massive sign, and I needed to act on it, and fast.

So I made a decision for me.

I made a decision for every ghostee out there—I was going to face my ghoster and take the power back.

If my story could help others, then I would push aside my fears and do it.

And I did.

I told Zuko that I would come with him and confront Ghost the next time he went to the gym.

And this right here was me taking the power back.

I lost count of how many times I questioned my decision.

What would it achieve?

We had something incredible, but it ended…no sequel.

But it never was the end for me. Ghost never gave me closure. All he did was leave—period.

I was left with this emptiness I could never fill, and I hated it. I was raised to never quit and to always stand up for myself. So even though the thought of seeing Ghost again terrified me, this was happening.

I needed to know if what he said, if what he felt, was real. I needed to know that for this small moment in time, things were how they were supposed to be.

I don't know why I needed validation. Perhaps I didn't want to be played a fool. I don't know. All I knew was that I needed to see Ghost and ask him what happened.

I spoke to a few friends about it, and honestly, they were split right down the middle. Some said to confront him, while others asked what I hoped to achieve.

His silence was all the answer I needed.

And they were right.

But my pride wouldn't allow me to let it go.

What right did he have to end things the way he did? I was worth a lot more than being ignored. No, this was happening, and this was happening now.

I knew what this would do to me because this wouldn't end in a happy reunion. But it would give me answers, and I could only hope it would help me move on.

I am stubborn and tenacious, and I NEVER give up, which is why when Zuko said he was going into the gym in two weeks to talk to Ghost, I said I was going too.

I had two weeks to prepare, but this wasn't a conversation I could prep for. I knew the moment I saw Ghost, I would know.

I would know if what he felt was real. Or if he was playing me the entire time.

Switzerland was in and out of the picture; more out than in, I guess. My friends told me numerous times to just end it, but I couldn't. I liked him more than I should. There wasn't a precise moment when it turned, but I think I just liked him the entire time.

But his silence did hurt.

The lag between replies was answer enough because when a man wants a woman, the woman, she knows. But when a man takes hours to reply when you know he is replying to others, then it's usually time for a woman to walk away with her pride intact.

But liking someone makes you do some crazy things…

So I just accepted him floating in and out; one foot in, one foot out because soon, both feet would be far, far away as Switzerland wouldn't be here anymore.

However, seeing him was a nice distraction. He was always kind to me, and I needed that kindness because I knew that seeing Ghost may be far from nice.

I hadn't told Switzerland about Ghost. I don't know why. I honestly didn't think he'd care. He never suspected, or perhaps he did, and he trusted me. But being with him gave me the confidence in myself and also, that good men did exist…and Ghost was not one of them.

Ghost essentially love bombed me, fucked me, and then he left.

There is no other way around it. Regardless of the circumstances he faced, that is what he did. And that is why there was no fucking way he was getting away with it. I was in a position to right the wrongs of something that was out of my control. I wanted answers.

The more people I spoke to, the more common this practice of ghosting seemed to be. It seemed everyone had their own Ghost, and that really pissed me off.

Suddenly, I wasn't just doing this for myself; I was doing it for every person who was me. And that gave me the confidence to don my reddest lipstick and kick-ass pumps and walk into that gym like the queen that I fucking am.

The day came, and I was nervous. But I quashed my fears and remembered who I was—I was someone not to be fucked with.

Zuko texted when he was on the way to the gym, and I said I would meet him there a few minutes after. As much as I wanted Ghost to feel the same anguish I did when he left without a word, I asked Zuko to give him the heads-up that I was on the way. If he didn't want to see me, then I would respect his wishes.

This wasn't a surprise attack.

I wanted to give him the opportunity to decline seeing me even though he didn't deserve it.

I arrived at the gym and waited in the car.

I gave myself a pep talk.

I could do this.

I looked at myself in the mirror, and suddenly, I saw something I was damn proud of—I saw strength.

I was a lot stronger than I ever thought I was. Doing this took balls, so I walked into that gym with nothing but confidence in every step when Zuko gave me the green light.

There was a huge window I had to walk in front of, and I strutted my shit (think Julia Roberts in *Pretty Woman*; *"Big mistake! Big! Huge!"*) because I realized I did nothing wrong here. Ghost was the one at fault. The ghoster usually is.

So I opened the door with poise and grace, and when our eyes locked…I realized that everything was going to be all right.

Months of torment and tears all led to this moment, and it was my time to get the answers I deserved.

He looked so damn hot. I hated him. My feelings for him hadn't shifted an inch. If anything, seeing him made me realize how hard I had fallen. But I didn't let it show.

I smiled.

He smiled.

Nothing else existed but this.

"How are you?" he asked, still smiling.

"Good," I replied, willing my heart to calm down. "I thought it was you."

Ghost nodded, those inquisitive eyes watching my every move.

"Apparently, we're doing a photo shoot together? How do you feel about that?"

I didn't have time to skim around the edges. I needed to do this before my bravado died.

Ghost paused, appearing to weigh over my question. "I don't know how I feel about being on display for everyone to see. Self-confidence issues and all."

He spoke about that often when we were together. So I knew he was legit. But he didn't care about my self-confidence when he slammed the door in my face without a goodbye.

"How are we supposed to do a cover, considering you're not talking to me?"

He got it—loud and clear.

"We need to talk."

I replied with a stiff-upper-lip smile.

I was battling my emotions—I should be angry with him, and my head was, but my heart, that traitorous sentimental little bish…

His staff watched on intently as it was clear that something was still between us, and it was sure to burn anyone alive who stood by and watched.

He appeared nervous.

I wish that made me feel better.

It didn't.

It made me want to hug him.

But I slapped my own ass and said, "I can go."

"No!" He raised his voice, panicked as he froze to the spot. "Don't go."

Even Zuko arched a brow, surprised by Ghost's response to me leaving.

"I meant, I can come back. I don't want to encroach on your workspace," I clarified, secretly content he didn't want me to go.

Ghost shook his head. "Wait for me there."

He pointed at a table and chairs off to the side, away from the foyer and prying ears and eyes.

Zuko and I took a seat, and Zuko was looking at me with a what-the-fuck look plastered all over his face. Regardless, he had my back. I didn't tell him much, but he knew something was between us. I guess he didn't realize how much so until he saw us together.

Ghost came over and sat off to the side in front of me.

Zuko was to my right.

All I could smell was Ghost and his signature fragrance. It brought back memories which I wish would get amnesia and fuck right off.

Ghost was staring at me openly.

And I purposely ignored him.

Zuko took the floor and detailed what he needed for the shoot.

For the entire time, Ghost looked at me. He was still that alpha, which drove me wild. I watched him from my peripheral vision but gave him nothing.

But inside? Fuck me, inside, I was dying.

"Do either of you have a partner who would object to the shoot?" Zuko asked, catching me off guard.

I looked at Ghost.

He was to take the lead.

And when he nodded firmly, I got the answer I finally deserved.

"It won't be an issue for me," I replied softly, unable to process that Ghost was with someone else.

Yes, I had moved on too, but ouch, this fucking stung.

Zuko excused himself as he knew we had much to discuss.

I turned to look at Ghost.

It was just him and me.

At that moment, I knew why his ghosting me hurt; it hurt because I loved him. I had fallen in love with him without consent. Love didn't ask permission. It just made me fall and fall hard without an instruction manual, and I was just expected to know how to survive.

And now that I finally knew, I had to come to terms with the fact that he loved someone other than me.

I wanted a do-over.

"You owe me an explanation."

He nodded, eyes downcast as if needing time to gather his thoughts.

"I do."

Silence…

But no.

He had more than enough time to formulate a reply. He had WEEKS…so his silence wasn't going to fly.

"You just vanished. What happened? I was worried…" I couldn't express anger because all I felt was sadness.

The anger was still there, but my heart just hurt. It took precedence over all.

"I…I wasn't happy. I didn't like the person I was. I was lonely."

"What…happened?" I asked once again because that wasn't an excuse.

Every person on this earth feels that way in their lifetime—it's what they do about it and how they treat others that distinguishes them from the rest.

"I…I got back together with my ex."

"Ex-wife?"

He nodded, and he looked…I don't know what adjective to use.

Sad, perhaps?

While I was just numb.

"And you couldn't tell me this?" I ask because it's not that hard.

It's actually very simple.

He finally met my eyes, and all I saw was torture in his.

I was unmoved, however.

Those walls I spoke of? They were now a hundred feet high and made of nothing but barbed wire and electrified, just for good measure.

"I didn't want to hurt you. I don't like hurting people."

"You hurt me by not talking to me. You hurt me by ghosting me. You hurt me by doing the one thing I asked you not to do."

Again, he cast his eyes downward. "I know, and I'm sorry."

And there was that word I so desperately wanted to hear…

Sorry.

That word bears so much significance and represents so much.

But now that I've heard it, did I feel better?

Was the sadness and pain which plagued me for months finally about to go away? Would I leave here exorcised of the demons of love and be able to find my happily ever after?

The answer is, sometimes, no amount of sorrys can make anything okay.

Yes, closure is nice, but does it lessen the pain?

No, it does not.

And that's how I felt.

I still felt numb.

I still felt sad.

I still felt overcome with pain because I loved someone…but he didn't love me back.

No amount of sorrys will ever fix that because I guess the song rings true; it's too late to apologize.

"I don't like confrontation."

"Am I confronting you now?"

"No."

"I just don't understand how you could vanish like that."

"Ten years is a long time, as you know," he added as he knew all about my previous marriage. "Her family knows mine."

Blah, blah, blah…

I tuned out after this because all I heard was excuses. All I heard was Ghost using elaborate words when only a few would have sufficed, and they were: *I am selfish and dishonest, and would rather hurt you than hurt myself.*

There are no justifications for his behavior.

He knew what he was doing when he chose to ignore my many messages, messages that were filled with love. Messages that expressed my pain that he was MIA.

But he didn't care because he chose the easy way out instead of being a decent human being.

"She wanted to reconcile, and ten years…it's a long time."

"Yeah, you said that."

Each time he spoke, he just appeared sadder and sadder.

I didn't understand it.

Wasn't he back with her because he was unhappy without her? He certainly didn't look any happier now.

So I asked the inevitable. "Are you happy?"

He looked at me, really looked at me, and sighed; a long-winded breath.

"Umm…"

The pause and noncommittal response were answer enough.

A small part of me was pleased to hear that he wasn't happy—I hated that part. That part needed to say ten Hail Marys and repent for being such a shitty human being.

Why was he with her when it's apparent he was clearly unhappy?

I didn't understand this.

"Was everything you said a lie, then? Or was it genuine? Was it real? Were we?"

His expression softened. "Of course it wasn't a lie. It *was* real. My feelings were real. Everything was. I still wan—"

I waited for the punchline, but there was none.

It was real, but in the end, I wasn't enough for him…but that's okay because I realized something, and that was…I was too much.

Too much heart.

Too much kindness.

And too much love.

The simple fact is that Ghost didn't deserve me.

I wanted a man who wanted me as much as I wanted him.

I wanted a man who fought for me. Not someone who couldn't have the common decency to tell me he had rekindled with his wife.

That man is a man I do not want.

No woman should because, ladies…we deserve more.

We deserve our fairy-tale ending because…

We.

Are.

Worth.

It.

Ghost continued making excuses, but by this point, I was done.

Zuko came back and asked if everything was all right.

I nodded because I had checked out.

Zuko was still adamant about the cover, and honestly, I would do it for him if he wanted. He was able to bring me some sense of peace with Ghost, so I could do this.

"If you both agree to the cover, then we will have to do a screen test to make sure there's chemistry between the two of you."

I deadpanned Ghost, who grinned.

"Oh, there's chemistry there. Don't worry about that."

Again, that impious part of me celebrated because I was happy to know he felt this chemistry too. That chemistry was there the second our eyes locked and hadn't diminished. In fact, it was probably worse.

But what good would that do me?

He wanted to fuck me—great, but that doesn't mean he respected me.

It meant the total opposite, in fact.

It meant he had chemistry with someone who wasn't his wife.

Bad dog…

And I was raised better than that.

I folded my arms and gave him a stiff upper lip.

Zuko was talking, but I wasn't listening because I was looking at Ghost, the man who I allowed to consume my life.

Yes, he was still the hottest man I've ever seen. And his teeth were in fact still rather cute, which I did mention in a weak moment as he smiled at me. But now that I knew the truth, I looked at him in a different light.

Perhaps I took him off his pedestal and saw him for who he really was—a man who didn't fight for me.

He was still adamant that he was self-conscious and had body dysmorphia, which, again, I knew to be true as it was something he touched on often when we were together.

"I don't know why you want me on a cover. I'm not photogenic at all."

I scoffed because he was so photogenic it made me sick. I liked that he never believed it, though. He was such an oxymoron. He comes across as confident, but deep down, he was far from it.

The longer we spoke, the more comfortable he grew. That was something that remained the same. When together, there was never silence…oh, except of course when he ghosted me for weeks.

"My nails aren't painted black," he said, extending his hands out for me to see.

On instinct, I reached for them, and the moment we touched, I knew our feelings *were* real.

He gave me his hands, and I took the offering, touching him for the first time since he left me. The chemistry between us left me breathless, and I often needed to inhale deeply because it felt like I couldn't get enough air fast enough.

It was beyond ridiculous.

I asked why they weren't black, as it was something he knew I liked. I found it interesting he decided to bring this up. He knew I found his black-painted nails incredibly sexy, so to mention it confused me.

But that seemed to be a common thing when Ghost was involved.

He didn't move his hands away, and replied with a smirk, "I can't find a black nail polish that stays on."

Okay, now we were just engaging in small talk. Yet I couldn't stop.

"There are so many you can buy," I said, rolling my eyes playfully.

He simply smiled.

Our banter had never left.

Neither had our feelings, apparently.

But where did that leave me?

Confused, that's what.

I pulled my hand away because I could feel that gravitational pull threatening to drag me under once more. And I couldn't do that.

Zuko asked once more about the cover, and it was apparent that Ghost was mulling over the possibility of doing it. The thought of being pressed up against my ex in intimate poses was a little too much. But I wondered if perhaps we did this, would something change?

But what was there to change?

Ghost had made his choice, and he didn't choose me.

I needed to accept that.

Yes, it was a fucking slap to the face, but I came here for answers, and I got them.

Ghost was still fixed on his insecurities as to why he was in two minds about the shoot, but I set him clear as I stood, hinting our time was over.

"Let's be honest. No one will be looking at you. It's all about me," I said, tongue in cheek.

Those eyes smoldered as he didn't make it a secret that he still wanted me as much as I did him. "Ain't that the truth."

I needed to leave, like now.

We walked toward the exit, and everything came crashing down. This was the last time I would see Ghost as I had a feeling he wouldn't do the shoot. And when your gut talks to you, listen to it.

I committed this moment to memory because I would never have another like it ever again.

I remember his smell; he always smelled so good.

I remember how nervous and sad he appeared to say goodbye.

And I remember me letting him go.

I softly bumped my shoulder into his, as there was no way I was hugging him farewell. But he turned around and met me head-on. I couldn't push past him, as he was standing in my way.

The last alpha move he was to make.

We simply stared at one another, and I suppose it's because we both knew this was goodbye.

I wish this was a moment in the movies where the MCs realize love prevails all, and they live happily ever after. But this was real life. It was my life, and I knew I had to write the closing line to our turbulent love story.

He stepped forward and hugged me tight. "Take care."

I was lost in his arms.

I was lost in who Ghost was.

I was lost to the man who made me feel something when I thought I was dead inside. And although our story didn't end how I wanted, it ended.

I wasn't left wondering.

I was no longer a ghostee.

I was a survivor.

Not a casualty.

And now, it was time for me to heal.

"You too," I whispered, eyes closed as I said goodbye to the boy I loved.

And *that's* how our story ends…

Life is a fucking ride.

Up and down.

Side to side.

We don't know what's coming our way.

I thought Switzerland had checked out, but it's funny because living this life, *my* life, one would think I was the decider of my own fate. But that's not how life works. It seems as though we're in the passenger seat, watching life take turns we don't want to take.

Switzerland was leaving in fifteen days.

I knew it.

He knew it.

He was chilled.

I was not.

His leaving hit me one night, and I just cried.

I cried because Switzerland showed me that good men did exist. He was everything I wanted, yet he was leaving forever.

We grew closer, which is against the sensible rules he laid down. But being with him was as innate as breathing. I didn't have to try. We often lay together in silence, and it wasn't uncomfortable.

It was still.

He would know something was wrong, however. He would often ask what caused my many sighs when I was deep in thought. Or asked what I was thinking when I was quiet.

He just knew.

I don't know how he knew.

He just did.

I often caught him looking at me and asked what he was looking at.

He would just smile.

The memories I have of him are ones I will cherish for the rest of my days. Even though he occupies such a small time in my life, his impact was so vast.

The times we spent in his room or mine were ones of happiness and laughter.

He shared so much with me.

Trust is a beautiful thing. I honestly think it is one of the most purest things in the world.

So when Switzerland opened up and told me things about himself that explained who he was, and why he acted the way he did, I just fell even harder for him.

There wasn't an exact moment.

There never is.

Because love hits you when you least expect it…and we're *never* ready for the fall.

Those days leading up to him leaving, we spoke about a lot. We spoke about absolutely everything. There's a turning point in the time you spend with someone when things just become natural, and that's how I felt with Switzerland.

I told him about Ghost and Mr. J. He simply listened, letting me spew forth my tragic past, only to hug me when I was done.

The more time I spent with him, the more I liked. But there was always the big fat elephant in the room—he was leaving.

I wanted to tell him to stay so many times. But I didn't want to be selfish. I knew what I was getting myself into from the moment we met. He never lied to me and was always upfront. I understood why he set down those rules.

But it didn't matter.

When someone tells me not to do something, I do the opposite.

Everything between us became more intense, and I guess that's what happens when you let someone in.

He would read my facial cues.

I would read his.

I would live for his hands around me when he pulled me close and kissed the back of my shoulder.

I died small deaths when he would say, "That's my girl."

Switzerland was loyal.

He was honest.

But I never knew how he felt.

And I guess he didn't know how I felt either.

Each second was counting down to ugly tears, and Mötley, she told me I had to tell him. I had to tell him how I felt. She said even once, just tell him that you don't want him to go.

But I couldn't.

That was selfish. And I hated myself that that was exactly how I felt.

I knew he was leaving.

So perhaps I could tell him because I would want to know if the tables were turned. I wasn't expecting anything in return. I just needed him to know how I felt.

So just how words have done my entire life, they saved me once more.

I wrote him a letter, expressing how I felt.

It was scary because regardless of feelings, I knew it wouldn't change the reality that he was going. But that's not the reason I wrote it. I wrote it because I never wanted any regrets with Switzerland. He was something special. And I had to say goodbye.

No matter how hard I tried, I could never keep him.

But you know what? It would be okay because as long as he was happy pursuing his dreams, I could live with why I had to let him go.

I was fighting a losing battle but it didn't make a difference, he was worth it to me.

Switzerland's response to the letter was mixed.

I left it on his doorstep with a gift I had bought. I didn't want to be there when he read the letter because I knew what his response would be.

He sent me a text early the following morning thanking me for the gift. He asked when a good time to call would be.

Um, never…

But he called because Switzerland wasn't a coward. He never ran away. He always stepped up to the plate, regardless of how tough things were.

Switzerland always preferred talking on the phone. While I prefer text. I guess with him being a musician and hearing the music, this may be why. And me, being an author, I speak better through written words.

I don't think I've ever spoken to anyone more on the phone than Switzerland. Looking back, I actually miss it.

We spoke about the letter, and I told him this was on me. I knew what I had signed up for. He was caring and kind, not wanting to hurt me. He explained about his walls and why they were in place. He knew he was leaving and that's why he didn't get attached.

He wasn't inconsiderate of my feelings. On the contrary. But he also made me feel a little the fool. Was I in denial this entire time together? Had I misread the times we shared?

Not what a romance author wants to hear, but it was the truth.

He could have ghosted me.

He could have made it weird.

But he didn't.

In his usual manner, he laid it all out on the table. Although it wasn't the response I wanted, it was better than no response at all.

I still didn't know how he felt, and when I questioned him, he gave me an analogy in true Switzerland style.

It made me laugh.

But it also made me sad.

Switzerland was right boy, wrong time. And the reality of it was it would probably never be the right time for us because he made it clear that he was never coming back.

So what to do…

The sensible thing would be to end things then, but he was leaving in seven days. What more damage could be done in seven days?

A lot…

The next day was our shoot for *LOVE HARD*.

Back up a moment.

In case you hadn't guessed, that boy on the cover is my Switzerland. I asked him to do the shoot with me because I didn't want anyone else to do it. Even though we weren't together, I would never look back at our pictures with regret.

Only happy memories to how he once made me feel.

It was about five billion degrees; the first hot day in forever. I got my hair and makeup done. I was excited to shoot with Switzerland. He made it clear he only was comfortable showing arms and hands. I was okay with whatever he was happy with.

Bunny called and asked if we could push the time out to later because it was too hot in the studio. It made sense.

But I knew Switzerland was on a tight schedule, organizing things before he left.

I asked if he could do later, and he said not really.

I understood, but again, it felt as though I had dedicated my time to someone who put me second best. I asked if there was a way he could make it work.

He said no and that I had this.

He was short on the phone, something he never was.

My stomach dropped when he hung up, wishing me the best.

I don't know what just happened, but I didn't like it.

I couldn't help but feel this response was because of the letter.

How could I be so wrong time and time again?

I didn't understand why my track record with men was so bad. But I honestly thought Switzerland was different. However, he knew how important this was to me, yet here I was, questioning what the fuck I was doing for the past few months.

But a minute later, my phone rang.

It was Switzerland.

And when I answered, he proved to me what I always knew to be true—he was the real deal.

"I can do it later. Come over now, and we can chill until the shoot."

That was Switzerland's favorite word—chill.

And that's what he always was. He was calm and always greeted me with a smile on that goddamn beautiful face.

And that was the case when I arrived at his house, and he greeted me at the door, just how he always did with a big smile on that face, which I was going to miss so very much.

We hugged big, and I thanked him for doing this for me. I knew he was strapped for time, but he sacrificed his plans for me.

It meant a lot.

The shoot wasn't for a few hours, so we "chilled."

I wanted to address the letter face to face, and he said something that resonated profoundly.

"I'm sorry I can't be your Prince Charming."

I don't know why, but those words still make me sad. They remind me of what we could have had.

Love ♡ HardER

I said he was a good man.

He said I was a good woman.

There was never a lack of affection between us. There was always just the fact that he was going.

We spent hours in his room, just how we always did

Talking.

He offered me his hand, always in constant touch.

The night was warm, and we lay on his bed together. It was something I will always remember because it's in the simplicity that I find so much.

When the time to shoot came, I looked at my boy and was so thankful for him. He was so damn hot, and when we were told to pose, he grabbed me how he always did and took charge.

The chemistry can't be faked. That's evident in every single shot. That's the reason I wanted to shoot with him. I knew this would be conveyed. So every expression, every placement of our hands, every goddamn look, it's who we are.

It's how we feel—and you can't fake that.

I loved dozens of the images, but the one I chose means so much to me because it's us. The look on his face reminds me of so much. There's a reason to it, and that reason is written all over that beautiful face.

Being this way with someone is rare for me because I don't usually connect this way.

Yes, Ghost affected me, but this was different. I wish I could explain how so, but being with Switzerland just felt natural.

He always seemed to know where to catch me so I wouldn't fall, and I mean that in every sense there is.

He wasn't overly affectionate, but he was in his own way.

The shoot captured some beautiful moments, ones which are forever encapsulated in time. And I wanted to share that with you.

An hour shoot ended up being almost twelve hours. That's how long we spent together. Switzerland was so strapped for time, but he put aside time for me because that's who he was.

He never asked for anything in return.

Never.

It was quite late after the shoot. I hadn't even driven for two minutes before he told me to pull over and he would drive home. Always the one in control. But I liked it. He always made me feel safe.

I snapped a photo of us—his hand on my thigh.

Again, it's the simplicity that I appreciate, and I will always remember the feel of his hand on my skin.

Just as I'll always remember his lips pressed to the back of my shoulder as he kissed me, holding me tight.

Being with him was effortless.

The night came to a close with a kiss goodbye.

Only six more to go…

The days leading up to Switzerland leaving were like any days before it.

I knew he was going, but I guess nothing really changed between us, so perhaps ignorance is bliss. He messaged and called me as usual, explaining his day, just as he always did.

Even though each moment was slowly ticking down to the inevitable, I didn't dwell on it. I knew he was leaving. My head accepted it. My heart, however…

Switzerland was leaving on Thursday. It was now Tuesday.

He called me and told me to come see him after he finished seeing his brother and friends.

The day had arrived. Was I prepared?

Not at all.

The moment I pulled into his driveway, he opened the gate and greeted me as he always did.

With that big smile.

He gave me a kiss on the lips, just how he always did, and we walked inside.

His house was packed up with only a few things remaining.

I looked at the place where many memories were made and felt my heart sink. This was really happening, and I was not prepared.

We spoke for a while before we went into his room.

He'd sold his bed, but he had a spare mattress set up on the floor. I took off my shoes, just how I always did, before getting into my side. He did the same.

He had mentioned a while ago that my side of the bed smelled of me and the cream I used to massage him with. It touched me at the time, but now, it just made me so sad. This was the last time I was to lay on my side of the bed with the man I had fallen for.

Where's the justice in that?

We lay together and spoke how we always did. He was excited to move. He was also anxious and overwhelmed because uprooting your life is a big thing.

I listened, savoring each moment spent together because they were soon becoming our last.

Again, the entire time we lay in his bed, he ensured I touched him. I will always remember him for that. My boy who was insistent that I didn't break down any walls was the one who always offered me his hand.

I asked if he showed his family our photos. He said he had. I didn't think he spoke about me to his family, or anyone, in fact, but he said something which proved otherwise.

He had mentioned that a family member had said I had been so nice to him. I don't know why, but it touched me so. It proved that he did speak about me, and the things he had said were all spoken in kindness.

Switzerland never really opened up, but this showed me that he did feel something for me—he may not have wanted to admit it, but I like to believe I affected him as much as he affected me.

The inevitable loomed, and he was the one who said it first. He was the one who said what I couldn't.

"I'm going to miss you."

My heart ached, and I forced back my tears.

I turned onto my side and replied, "I'm going to really miss you. This sucks."

Silence before he bent down to hug me.

Switzerland said some beautiful things. It was all encouraging and promising for our futures, but a future lived apart.

It hurt because he always had an endgame.

He was focused on leaving.

And me, all I wanted was for him to stay.

He wanted me to know that what we shared wasn't just physical. That it extended beyond that. It was nice to hear that he liked hanging out as much as I did. And that's the reason it was so hard to say goodbye.

To connect on all levels is a rare thing.

He made me laugh.

He made me hot.

He made me feel safe.

He was so much, yet I always felt like what we had was never enough.

He tried to lighten the mood by saying he was the one who got away.

I told him to get over himself.

But he was right.

"You're never going to find a man like me," he said with a smile. "You'll never find a man who will sing to you on cue like I do."

And he was right.

The more comfortable you grow with someone, you begin to build your own little world. And that's what we did.

One day, I asked him something, and when he didn't reply, I said, "Yes? No? Maybe?"

And without warning, he broke out into a theme song from a TV show.

Love ♡ HardER

It was a long song too, and each time, he ensured he sang every word to it. It made me laugh. So he made sure he never missed a word.

It was our thing.

He said if I was ever sad or needed to talk, all I needed to send him was those three words, and he would sing to me.

It really was a beautiful thing.

"You'll be on a date with a man, and he's eating a steak, and you'll say, so do you like your steak? Yes? No? Maybe? And his response will be yeah, I guess."

I laughed, but to think of myself on a date with someone other than him made me sad.

I reminded him that I was a vegan, not that he could forget. But the analogy made me laugh.

There are no words to ever express goodbye to the person you don't want to go.

I said to him, "So what are your parting words? How does our story end?"

I was curious.

He hugged me tight and said, "It's not going to be the song."

He knew me too well.

"You're just going to have to wait until I say goodbye. But this isn't goodbye. You're going to see me again."

That's what everyone says.

But distance changes so much.

He said so many things to me to ensure I would be okay. That we would see one another again and that we'd always be in one another's lives.

And perhaps we would be. But it wouldn't be in the way I wanted, and I wondered if maybe cutting him lose would be the easier thing to do.

Cold turkey.

If I can't have all of him, then I don't want him at all.

I didn't want to hold on to pieces when I wanted the whole thing.

It's too hard to love someone from afar.

He wanted me to live my life and wished me all the happiness I deserved.

"Thank you for crossing the moat to meet me outside your castle walls," I said, and I meant it.

That's the analogy he used to explain why he didn't get attached. So many walls built around my boy. I wish I had more time because even though he always said he wished he could be my Prince Charming, if time was on our side, then I think I could have slayed his dragons because I didn't need a Prince Charming. I didn't need saving.

All I wanted was my king to rule alongside his queen.

He smiled. "I crossed the moat to meet you, but now, it's time to retreat back into the castle."

I could feel the tears approaching.

It was time…

I put my shoes on, and he waited for me in the living room.

Once my laces were tied, I took one last look around the room and committed it to memory because I knew I would never be here again.

Switzerland wouldn't be back. He was too stubborn not to succeed. He would throw everything at his new life, and I knew he wouldn't give up. A trait of his I always admired.

Now, it just hurt.

It's amazing how a place can affect you so.

Or a smell.

Or a hole in the wall where the possum once lived.

Or even a spilled coffee stain on the curtain.

All of these little things mark that particular moment or place special because they will always remind you of a moment in time. A moment you can never relive.

I would never make any new memories with Switzerland, so I ensured to hold on to the ones I made with him in this very room.

We laughed a lot.

We spoke for hours.

He called me his girl as he kissed my shoulder.

No new memories would ever be made in this room again.

No matter what anyone says, no one is ever ready to say goodbye to someone they don't want to let go. But I left his room with a happy sadness in my heart.

There was silence between us as he walked me to his door. He complimented me on my shoes.

"So sparkly," he said, and all I could do was smile.

It's funny the things we remember when something monumental is about to happen. I'm certain so much more was said, but him talking about my shoes made me happy because he knew how much I love my shoes.

I wasn't ready.

But the truth is, I never would have been.

He opened the door, and we walked outside.

I turned around to hug him tight, the words stuck in my throat.

"You're going to live in your house by the sea," he said, a dream of mine I had shared. "You're going to kill it. I know it."

Tears stung my eyes. "Thank you for being so beautiful. My beautiful boy. I'm going to miss you so much."

"Likewise," he said softly, hugging me tight. "I'm going to miss you too. I'll call you from the airport."

"Safe travels."

I let him go forever, and my heart, fuck me, my heart was heavy with regret.

I wanted to say more, but there will never be enough words to say goodbye to someone you wanted to love but never could. I looked at him one final time, thankful to have met someone as incredible as him.

I didn't see Switzerland off at the airport.

I wanted to, but it just didn't happen.

I texted him in the morning, and he sent a message back.

Nothing had changed.

I told him I missed him.

He said he missed me too.

I tried to keep busy during the day, and how I did that was by writing what you're reading right now.

Words, they're so powerful.

The only way to properly express how I feel is to have you live through my words in real time. The pain was heavy in my heart, and when I saw my phone ring, the caller being Switzerland, I knew this was really it this time.

He called just as he was about to board. The gesture was so reflective of him.

Always kind to me. Always showed he cared.

He told me about his final day, and we spoke how we usually would.

He said his goodbyes to family and friends, and I could hear they were bittersweet. It's always hard to leave the ones you love behind, even if a bright future is ahead.

I didn't want our last goodbye to be tainted with sadness, so I asked him about his plans.

He was ready.

He said something that resonated. Rather, it was what he didn't say that touched me.

"I just thought I'd call you and say…"

A very long pause.

He finally opted for, "Have a good week."

I always wondered what he wanted to say as I don't think have a good week was it.

But in the silence, we can fill in the blanks, and like a choose-your-own-adventure story, I choose to believe he wanted to say he'd miss me too. That being together was fucking incredible, and that we will always share something special.

Sometimes silence speaks volumes, and this was one of those times.

We spoke some more, never any uncomfortable silences. Never a goodbye lingering on the horizon, and I realized that was because this wasn't goodbye.

Perhaps a goodbye for now?

One can only hope.

As he spoke, it reminded me that I was so glad to have taken a chance on the man who changed my life profoundly.

He said we would speak all the time, and he would let me know when he arrived. It was as if nothing was different, but we both knew that wasn't true.

The announcements sounded over the speakers, as it was time to board.

I wished him a safe flight and thanked him for calling, as it meant a lot.

And his parting words were so typical of my boy. Always thanking me. Always grateful for me being in his life.

"Thanks for everything. I'll talk to you soon. Bye."

And that was it.

He has a quote tattooed on his arm, and after getting to know him, I realized how appropriate it is. He worked hard. He had big dreams. He is chasing what he wants in life, and I admire him for not being a slave to the grind.

This is one of the many reasons I fell so hard for him.

He is driven and focused on achieving his dreams. So how can I be bitter about that?

I can't.

I'm sad, yes, of course I am, but knowing he left to challenge himself and grow takes guts. He didn't want comfortable. He wanted to explore what this life had to offer him.

I know, dear reader, you may be wishing for something a little more dramatic. Perhaps he never left.

But he did.

His parting words weren't climactic, but they were him. He didn't make a fuss. He didn't express his undying love for me because this was never going to end that way.

I knew that.

But the fact he assured me we would speak just how we always did makes me have faith that perhaps he would stick true to his word, and we will forever be in one another's lives. And I believe in one way or another, we will.

It's been over six months since Switzerland left, and although I wanted to end his chapter on a different note, I thought it was only fair to bring some kind of…closure, perhaps.

Switzerland and I spoke like we normally did when he first moved. Things weren't easy for him, and moving proved to be quite the challenge. But he of course made it work, just as I knew he would.

He called me often in the beginning. I had hope.

But with time, he began to fade into the shadows, and he soon felt like a dream. He became a distant memory, and I wonder if this was because my heart was trying to cope. I tried to keep in contact, but he fed me the bare minimum.

I felt like I was the one making all the effort. He was settling into his new life. I understood. I knew this was destined for us. But as the weeks gave way to months, Switzerland became white noise, and I lost sight of him. He would occasionally check in by being present in my socials, but any actual conversing stopped.

When the cover of *LOVE HARD* released, he sent me a congratulatory message.

It was so…curt.

Unlike what I expected a past lover to send.

Mötley and Sparkles had told me to detach. But goddamn, he still affected me.

The messages were so scarce between us. It made me sad when he did message as it was a reminder of what we shared.

I didn't want this weirdness between us. I didn't want it to taint the happy memories I had of him. So I sent him a message, not really sure of the aftermath.

It went something along the lines of: *You speak to me like we never kissed...*

He replied as I knew he would.

I know, but we're 15,000km apart, my darling woman. What am I supposed to do?

That's just a number... I typed back.

He never replied.

And it's okay.

There wasn't anything he could say. It was fact. It was something I knew from the beginning.

So I wish I could present a happier ending. But that's not how life works.

He still checks in with my socials. As I do with his.

There really isn't much we can do as we both agreed that long distances don't usually work.

So it feels as though we're both a ghost in one another's life, watching from afar but never getting too close.

I don't know what the future holds for us, but I do hope we will see one another again. I don't think it will be the same as those simpler times in what feels like a lifetime ago, but I do know that I will never regret meeting him.

He is doing so well in his new life, and that's all I ever wanted for him.

So the question is, will Switzerland and I see one another again?

Yes?

No?

Maybe?

I love your dimples.

DIMPLES

I should have learned my lesson.

You've read my tragic love affair with love. I should have just accepted that love and I were destined to speak different languages without Google Translate on hand.

I realized early on that I was okay with sitting by myself in a restaurant or a cinema; I didn't need someone to complete me because I was content on my own.

My divorce forced me to relearn how to be human again in a sense. When you've spent over a decade with someone, you lose a sense of who you are. Well, that's how I felt anyway. But I didn't mind. I did this because of…love.

That asshole.

So newly single, the world was my oyster and blah blah…but half the time, I felt as though I was thrown into the deep end and expected to know how to swim. I can't, by the way. But as we know, love doesn't care what we can or can't do.

I tried my best and made a lot of mistakes. But I'm at the age where I like to see my mistakes as lessons learned, so when I met a younger man, I should have guessed he was a lesson that was about to grip me by the throat and choke the good sense right out of me.

We all know where this is going…

Dimples was a lot younger than me. Like a lot. I know they say age is only a number, but from the get-go, I knew I couldn't keep him. And more importantly, he wouldn't want to be kept.

He had that something, something that I go goo goo gaga over. I don't know what it is. I get asked often how do I know.

I just do.

It was the same with the other men you've read about.

You just know.

And I knew with Dimples that he was going to break me, and I was going to fucking relish every second of it because I'm clearly a masochist.

I wasn't looking for anything, not after Switzerland.

But I wasn't looking for him either when I met him. And sometimes, that's when the best stories unfold.

He was the one who saw me first, but the moment I took note of that twisted smirk and those incredible colored eyes, I couldn't look away. He was confident and made the first move. I liked what he was throwing down.

He was witty and polite, but always, in the background, there were cheerleaders, waving their pom-poms, chanting… *roses are red, violets are blue, if I had a brick, I'd throw it at you.*

He knew I was older. He told me he liked older women. He told me I was so attractive to him. He asked questions and seemed genuinely interested.

So what's the issue here?

Roses are red, violets are blue, if I had a brick, I'd throw it at you.

I knew that regardless of how our beginning commenced, this would end in ugly tears. I predicted the plot twist from just reading the prologue.

I needed to run away…which is why I did the opposite.

Dimples was supposed to be a cookie, but I knew from the moment we kissed, the only cookie I would be having was in my gallon of vegan ice cream I would be crying into when things ended.

Dimples was my "type."

I didn't think I had a type, but alas, here we are.

He was tall, dark hair, and his eyes a golden hazel. He was big; I always felt shadowed in his arms. I really liked that. Perhaps because of our ages. Or maybe it's because I am constantly looking for my Superman.

He smelled good.

He tasted good.

He was good.

Period.

He sent a lot of messages and voice notes early on. And yes, there is such a thing as being attracted to someone's voice. His South African accent would occasionally come through, making me want to die small deaths and not helping the predicament at hand.

I tried to convince myself that he was just a cookie and not to get attached. But the more we spoke, the more I saw what a fucking liar, liar, pants on fire I was.

The main thing I liked about Dimples was that he didn't seem to realize how gorgeous he was, which surprised me because, at first glance, I got *whispers* fuckboy vibes.

But the more we spoke, the more it became clear he was quite humble. However, fuckboy he may not be (jury was still out) but party boy he was. He acted the way any young man at his age was "expected" to act when with friends.

And that's what always reminded me of his age.

It was the slap of reality I needed to exorcise myself of these demons and save myself the tears.

Oh, hindsight, how you can fuck right off on the shitty horse you rode in on.

We spoke for a few days, and I tried to remember why he was bad for my sanity. But with anything, things that want to kill me make me feel most alive, and when he dropped a few comments which showed me that he's an alpha by nature, I waved goodbye to good sense. She was a party pooper anyway.

He suggested we meet.

It's also suggested to read instructions. As it is not to touch something hot as it'll burn. But here I was, stripping off clothes as I ran toward a raging inferno.

He messaged a lot, but they always do in the beginning, something I learned the hard way. So I was skeptical. I hated that I viewed any new human connection this way, but history scarred me, and those scars will never heal.

There were many things I liked about Dimples. He never presumed. He never crossed the dick pic line. He never was crass. He was clear about what he wanted, and that was me. But he never resorted to dirty talk to elucidate that.

He was honest and expressed that he was attracted to me and wanted to meet to explore that attraction in person.

My head and my heart are on two entirely different realms. My head knew this is the worst idea I've had in a very long time, but my heart was donning a pair of red glitter pumps while pursing her red lips.

Needless to say, my head exited the room with her middle fingers raised.

We planned a day to see one another, but I was surprised as he was the one who canceled early on.

Note to reader: you have the advantage here, as I went into this blind. But please remember this as it's pivotal to the story.

His excuse was he had to help his friend as he was getting his dog desexed.

Yes, I scratched my head too.

But I figured he was like most men; they talk up a big game, but none of them actually deliver. So I assumed Dimples was just like the rest. I was surprised, however, because he had said he liked older women, and most older women I know wouldn't stand for this sort of shitty behavior.

I wasn't disappointed. I was surprisingly numb. I hate that that's how I am.

I guess being burned one too many times has, in fact, taught me something.

I accepted that Dimples was just another man who could be added to the DNF list.

However, when he messaged and said he could now come over, I was surprised once again. Was he playing games with me? Testing me to see if I was someone who would accept sloppy seconds?

I told him I wasn't available because I wasn't. I may not have had plans with someone else, but I had plans with my self-respect. There was no way I was setting this precedence early on. This wasn't okay, and I wanted him to know that.

He apologized and said that he wanted to see me, but he had also agreed to help out a friend. He seemed genuine. He also sent many voice messages reiterating that he wanted to see me.

In the end, I believed him.

His voice didn't betray any deceit. So I agreed to see him two days later.

Oh, dear reader, your narrator clearly has amnesia when it comes to cute boys.

We both knew where this was headed, so I asked him to bring some protection. Safe sex is important. He made a comment that I liked; he hadn't presumed sex was on the agenda.

I honestly wasn't expecting much, and that's when most of my troubles begin. The moment I opened my door, I got the same feelings I did with every other man who left me brokenhearted.

Oh boy...

It didn't help that the opening line he fed me was, "I believe I owe you something." In which he gripped my chin and kissed the ever-living fuck out of me.

We all know where this is headed...

We had amazing sex, the kind of sex where you just lose yourself and forget your own name kinda sex.

I was so screwed in every literal way that there was.

Once I got the feeling back in my legs, we spoke for a very long time. It surprised me. I thought this was just supposed to be a hookup. So why was he still here? And why was he making conversation?

He stayed for hours. We spoke about lots of things. He was so articulate. He was also very driven. I picked up on that early on. I could feel myself going down that fucking rabbit hole again.

We had sex again.

Better than the first time.

Yup, this was headed for heartache and tears.

Once he left, I wrestled with what to do. I knew this couldn't lead anywhere. Regardless of his maturity, he was at the beginning.

While me? I felt like I was somewhere in-between.

The next day, he messaged, and of course it wasn't a "hey, what's up."

Oh of course not.

It was an *Ican'tstopthinkingaboutyouandneedtotasteyouagain* kinda message. The type of message that makes you swoon and swoon hard because he felt it too.

He sent voice messages and pictures. He did everything at the beginning that made me believe that perhaps he was different. Perhaps he was the unicorn we're all seeking to find.

I write that with a bittersweet smile because that's what Dimples said I was: a unicorn. He said the hotter the girl, the crazier they are. I didn't really understand this analogy until he sent me a video explaining this principle the next day.

Now I see that the reason a woman may seem "crazy" to a man is because most men push us to the point of insanity where we explode, frustrated by their mixed signals. Or radio silence. Or the fact they think it's okay to love bomb us until they move on to the next thing without being honest.

It was New Year's a couple of days after Dimples came over, and yes, I had a New Year's kiss that rocked my world. He was tall, Irish, and kissed me until I forgot my own name.

I was surely cured from the Dimples curse.

Oh, how I wish that were true.

Dimples continued to chase hard, sending messages that cemented my fate.

Fuck, I want you so bad. This is never going to end. I want to fuck you every day, and I want you to miss how my cock feels in you.

Can we see a pattern here?

Sound a little reminiscent of what Ghost sent?

But I ignored the warning signs because I didn't want to see them. I wanted to believe he was different.

He left for a different state early on in the year for work. He was only supposed to be gone for two weeks. He was gone for close to seven.

I was certain things would eventually fizzle, and we'd forget about one another.

How wrong I was.

He sent so many messages when away. I didn't understand it. He didn't owe me anything, yet he messaged me every single day. Some smut, but mostly, messages that expressed how much he missed me and that what he felt was solid.

Every day, he told me he wanted me so bad and that he missed me.

To keep the fire burning bright, he sent me the hottest videos. Ones which I am sure you can use your imagination for.

He said often that he never wanted anyone as badly as he did me. That he never wanted to stop what he had. He jerked himself off thinking of me, and that he didn't want anyone other than me.

He often recalled memories of our night together, and I liked that he did that. I liked that he thought about what we did.

He said he never wanted to stop this and that he was all mine.

He was sad to be away for so long and often went off-grid. When I would question where he was, he would come back and explain that although not the best communicator, he was still here.

And I believed him.

He didn't give me a reason not to.

He told me all he wanted was to come home to me.

We exchanged so many messages during his time away. I asked so many questions, all of which he answered without fail.

I asked what his three vices are, and his answer just killed me, smalls.

My first vice...is my lust for you.

He always sent me pictures of himself saying he wanted me, that he was thinking of me, or that he was away from me for too long. He would occasionally send drunken messages, professing how much he missed me. They do say the truth comes out when one is drunk.

Every morning, he sent a good morning message.

He interacted with my socials, giving me a nudge that he was there.

It was so much.

Not once did I ever doubt his "feelings" for me.

That is, until one day, he was back, as in back home, only an hour away from me home.

He didn't tell me he was coming home, which I thought was odd. I mean, we had only been talking about his return for weeks, and now that he was back, there was radio silence.

He posted stories on his socials, and I anticipated that he would hit me up with a time when he was coming over.

But I waited…and waited…and nothing.

He was down for the weekend, and before I knew it, he was flying back out.

I was confused. Had I dreamed up the entire affair? I mean, he was home and didn't even message that he was back.

We all know what this is. But for those viewers at home, let me spell it out for you.

RED FLAG…

He was waving that motherfucker early, but here we are…

When I asked why he didn't let me know he was back, this was his reply:

Hey baby xx Sorry, been so much going on with house and stuff. I can maybe see you before I go to the airport.

Blink.

Blink. Blink.

This was the time I should have hit the road and thanked him for the memories. But he fed me such believable bullshit, I went against everything I stood for and stayed.

I wrote back.

If you're not interested, please just tell me.

No, I am!!! I have been working for so long, and I've been really busy with this weekend with stuff back home. I just haven't found the time yet (insert sad face)

He sent a voice message when I went quiet, apologizing if I got the wrong idea. He wanted to see me and he definitely would when he got back.

I gave Dimples so many outs, but he never took them.

He stayed away for many more weeks, and our "situationship" continued. But I noticed he was beginning to retreat.

Perhaps we should leave it here?

I feel so bad. I never thought I'd be gone so long. We don't have to leave it there 😔

It's a little hard to keep the momentum going when I don't know when you're coming back. Or if you don't talk anymore. This is why I keep asking where your head's at because I don't know what's going on 😔

I feel so bad now 😔 it's been so crazy, I swear. Babe I'm still here, I just have so much going on with work and I'm exhausted mentally. Nothing has changed at all. I will try better to communicate more. That's my fault. I dream about seeing you again. And it will happen again. I miss you so much x I think I will be back end of the week but when I land I will come see you for a bit. How does that sound? And we can catch up and talk.

These are examples of our text message ping-pong while he was away.

When he would withdraw, I would ask what's wrong and he would come back with such heartfelt messages. Surely he was legit. No one puts that much effort into someone if they weren't serious, right?

I like to believe at the time he meant every single word.

From talking to friends who have experienced the same thing, we all agree that yes, boys do mean and believe the things they say at the time. But it's their actions afterward that matter.

Things were back to being good. It was a common theme for Dimples and me.

We were good for a week or so, then there was radio silence and I questioned every single thing.

Another common occurrence was Dimples coming home for the weekend without telling me.

This happened four or five times. I honestly lost count.

Yet I stayed.

I made excuses for his shitty behavior because I…I honestly don't know why.

There were so many times I should have seen Dimples for who he really was. A people pleaser. A coward. A confused young man. A fuckboy.

I still don't know why he entertained "us" for as long as he did. He was more away than he was home. He wasn't getting sex, yet he stayed. He continued to insist he was interested and that nothing had changed and that he was coming home to me.

When he flew back out for work, and I didn't see him—again, I decided to lay it all out on the table. I couldn't take it. Not again. It was Ghost all over again.

The thing which confuses me is when you come home, you're MIA. But when away, you're attentive. Perhaps you're coming home and someone else is kissing your face; and I get it, it's been ages since we last saw one another, but for me, when I want someone, I don't forget to message them, I would let them know about my day, and I would let them know if I'm coming home. (I'm sure you said you were coming home over the weekend?) Lack of communication is a massive ick. I need it in every aspect—not just in the bedroom. I don't know if you're a dog or cat person, or if you can use chopsticks. I don't know all the random, fun stuff about you which is also important to me to balance out the physical. You may not be a big communicator, and that's okay. But just tell me that. Long story short, I still want you, it's just hard when you go quiet. Please just kiss me soon. Promise? x*

I'm a dog person and I can't use chopsticks but you can teach me. I fully understand everything. When I come home I'm exhausted and just want to sleep but I promise I'm coming home to see you in an intimate way sexually and personally. I'm sorry I suck at communicating. I want you. It's been so much for me with work. It's all over soon. I promise xx

Again, I wanted to include snippets of what my situationship was like with Dimples because this wasn't a casual thing for either of us. Well, I didn't think it was, not when he was sending me messages such as that.

I thought we were good and then once again, he magically appeared home for the weekend without telling me. This was the last time, however.

He was back for good—well, semi-good.

He was back for a week this time and he promised he would see me.

He sent so many voice messages and I could hear he was genuine. It's one thing to read something, but to hear the emotion in one's voice—there's no faking that. In case I was wrong, however, Mötley and Sparkles would hear and read every single thing he sent.

They also had a crush on him and believed him to be sincere.

So with him back, we were all set for a reunion which was months in the making. I was so happy to see him. He sent me a voice message mid-afternoon saying things were hectic at a course he was doing and he hoped he could make it.

My stomach dropped.

Then when my phone rung, I knew what was happening.

He wasn't coming.

Months of talking.

Months of flirting.

Months of him telling me he's coming home to me were all fucking lies.

I was sad.

But most of all, I was angry with myself for being so fucking stupid.

I was triggered as this was Mr. J and Ghost all over again.

He begged I be understanding of his situation. That he was under a lot of pressure and that he wanted to see me. He really did, but in the end, he never did.

He flew out—again for work a few days later.

I backed off because honestly, what was the point? And that's when he sent a message which again, friends, RED FLAG because now, we're venturing into fuckboy territory.

Hey b x

I'm coming back Wednesday night.

I'm coming to your house.

I want you that bad.

I miss you x

He was giving me the boyfriend experience and I wanted to believe this was real which, rookie move on my behalf. However, I ignored him because fool me once, shame on you, fool me twice…and I am done.

But he just chased harder until one day, I cracked. I honestly didn't understand what he wanted from me.

I asked if he had chemistry with other girls and his reply should have been the slap in the face I needed.

I have chemistry with you.

Warning bells because he answered my question in an indirect way. I didn't see it at the time, but now, I see that Dimples was just feeding me bullshit I wanted to hear. Did he mean it at the time?

Love ♡ HardER

I like to believe that he did. But the odds are not in his favor.

Can you guess the rest?

Wednesday came, but he didn't. I didn't even know he was back until I saw his socials.

By this stage, this was just humorous.

Mötley and Sparkles were as confused as me. Mötley was my forever angel when I felt defeated in every way saying he had fooled her too. That she was along for the ride this entire time and that he had her believing the shit he said. She too didn't understand what reason he had to lie.

So I asked what he wanted with me when once again, he wouldn't leave me alone.

He sent me a video of him blowing me a kiss.

Again, enough to keep me engaged without answering the question at hand. And we all know what this is—breadcrumbing.

I ignored him for a little while and as always, he came back.

Hey we will catch up soon!!! Like super soon. Much later tonight or next week? X I need to kiss that face xx

Again, that never happened.

Hey you, I'm still kinda sleeping off last night. I feel shit, but we can do next week during the week. I will come over and we can do whatever you want.

And did he? No, of course he didn't.

I had checked out weeks ago, but he wouldn't leave me alone. He would pester me and honestly, in the end, curiosity won because finally, the day arrived where he PROMISED, like really promised he would see me.

It was a Sunday.

I wasn't convinced because I knew he would be drinking Saturday night with friends, so he would be hungover come Sunday.

But he promised he would come.

Our birthdays were coming up. Two days apart. He looked up our star signs. What guy does that? No fuckboy puts in that much effort.

Sunday came and the inevitable happened.

I've had a big night. So I need to nap a little before I come see you if that's okay.

Of course, take your time.

I knew where this was headed.

I will probably be late tonight. I hope that's okay 🙄 like 8:30ish, is that okay?

Take your time. Kisses at the door please.

First thing I'm going to do. Trust me.

Two hours later: **I haven't slept I FEEL like a train wreck atm fuck me. I'll probably be late tonight. I hope that's okay.**

Late is fine, but I kinda knew this would happen. I don't want you doing something you don't wanna do because you'd be here if you wanted to be. What am I supposed to say? You tell me 'cause this is your call.

No I'm just really hungover trust me. I want it so bad. Trying to give myself enough rest xx

An hour later…

Can we do tomorrow night? I should have known I'd be too hungover today. I can come after work??

I had run out of words because I was humoring us both at this stage.

Okay x

Thank you. Please don't get confused. I fucking want to come. I should have known I was going to have a big night.

Honestly, I am very confused with what exactly you want from me. I can do about 8?

That will be fine. I'll come late tomorrow. I don't want to confuse you. I genuinely thought I'd be alright but feel like death and I want to make sure I am not half dead when I see you.

Did I believe him?

Yes.

Was I stupid for doing so?

Yes and no.

The reason is because when I say something, I stick to my word. My error here is trusting someone to do the same thing.

Sparkles and Mötley were as much involved in this situationship as I was. When I relayed the latest Dimples drama, they often referred to my situationship as "we."

"*We* need to remember he does this when away for work."

"When he does this, *we* need to say something."

They were a part of this as much as me because I needed them to validate that I wasn't reading into things. Or that I wasn't crazy. That he was genuine and not a lying asshole who was taking me for a ride.

Mötley once again said he fooled us all.

I felt a little better after that.

Without my friends, I hate to think where I would be because Dimples really emotionally and mentally screwed me. The reason being, I thought he was the real deal.

He put so much effort into "us."

What I've shared is merely a fraction of what he sent me on a daily basis. He promised so many times that he was mine. But he never was.

Cut to Monday, make that day ten billion and one.

My phone rung an hour before he was meant to arrive. He started the call with, "Promise me you won't get mad."

Goes without saying, I got mad.

He called knowing this would end in a fight and that's why I had respect for him for doing that. He could had texted. He could have ghosted. But the moment he called, he listened to everything I had to say and begged I forgive him.

At the time, I thought that showed he cared. But now, I just think Dimples just lived in Dimples's world and on Dimples's time.

I very bluntly told him on the phone why would I want to see him when he couldn't make the effort to see me. He said he understood that. It was evident in his voice that he didn't like confrontation. To be fair, he listened and reasoned with me until I hung up, frustrated with how he thought this was okay.

I could hear his friends in the background and I liked that he didn't shy away from speaking to me in front of them. I wasn't a secret and I know I wasn't when I saw one of his friends had viewed my socials. He had spoken about me to at least one of them.

But that didn't excuse his behavior.

The next day, I sent a message:

Why do you continue to make plans only to cancel?

He replied within seconds:

I'm not canceling deliberately. I couldn't make it Sunday so I tried my best to make it work Monday. Argh please just understand. I will have time this weekend. I'm sorry okay x

He sounded genuine…again.

So I said okay. And tried one last time…

That night, he sent so many voice notes saying he didn't mean to be frustrating, and he's just trying to be honest, and it's backfiring. He didn't want to make me angry and just ended up making me angry with him anyway.

He said I was to trust him. That he wanted to come over, and that he couldn't emphasize how badly he wanted to see me. He couldn't wait to see me when it happened, and it would. He promised.

Blah, blah…

Again, I retreated, ignoring him when he continued to chase, but when it was my birthday a few days later, he sent me a message that made me want to throw my phone out the window because I was slightly impressed that he had remembered my birthday.

Happy birthday, babyyyy. I hope you have the best birthday today, and I'll have a surprise for you this weekend.

He checked in throughout the day, asking what I was up to.

I gave him the bare minimum, but he just wouldn't quit.

It was his birthday two days later. So I sent a birthday message.

He insisted he wanted to see me Saturday, which was his actual birthday. I knew this wasn't going to happen, but he swore it would.

I asked what he wanted to do for his birthday, and he said he wanted to do me.

All the things a fuckboy would say.

Saturday came, and he did what I knew—he asked if we could catch up Sunday instead.

By this stage, I was so used to disappointment, I agreed. It's incredible the things we just accept after a while. He wore me down to the point of not expecting anything to stop myself from being disappointed.

But Sunday came, and, my friends, guess what happened? So did he—finally!

Surprised?

That makes us both.

It had been over three months since I saw him, and when he messaged me late that night, promising me he was coming, I believed him. I don't know why I did. You've read our history. But I think he knew if he canceled one more time, then we were done; like for real this time.

He messaged when he was on the way.

This was really happening, and there was no way I could prepare my heart for what was about to come.

The moment I saw him standing at my front door, I knew he was worth the wait because, my god, our chemistry was rampant.

We kissed how I thought we would.

Everything was so much more intense this time.

Something incredible and unexplained is shared between two people who connect in such a way. This is part of the reason I gave him so many chances. To share this connection with someone is rare for me. So when I do, I'm all in.

He touched me with tenderness and hunger.

He spoke dirty words, which only amplified our passion.

He always seemed so much older than his years. His experience in and out of the bedroom cemented this.

The craving didn't dissipate. It just continued to grow with each kiss, each touch. And I knew he felt it too.

Which is why I didn't understand why it took him so long to see me.

The sex was something else. He set the bar high, and that's not because he was an unbelievable lover. No, it's because he let me in.

He stopped with what he thought I wanted to hear and just was himself, someone I liked a lot. We spoke for hours and hours. Being with him felt natural, just how it did with the other boys I let in.

He promised he would see me before I left to go overseas.

He texted me when he got home. It was all very reminiscent of Ghost. But I chose to believe he was different.

He messaged the next day.

I don't know what I was expecting, but it was good. The connection was still there.

But then, day by day, I felt him pull back. I don't know how I knew; I just felt he was taking one step, then two, away.

I said I felt as though things have changed since the night we saw one another.

He asked why I thought that as he thought it was really good.

Okay, so maybe I was reading into things. I told him he was less vocal and that we've not made any plans to see one another again.

This is a trigger of mine, I know. This is on me. But he knew I wasn't interested in being pen pals.

I'm not trying to be less vocal at all. It can be very hard to see one another sometimes! 😳

And this was the beginning of the end…

As the day I was leaving approached, I asked if I would see him before I left.

Hey, I have work in the morning and a super full on weekend 😳

I didn't hear from him all weekend. He texted me the morning I left.

Love ♡ HardER

Hey, so sorry been a crazy weekend. When are you leaving? Is it today? x I hope you have the best flight and trip.

I flew overseas and got to work, keeping busy. Dimples kept in touch from time to time, but he was still distant. The shift was present. The tables were turned this time. I was the one away, but my feelings for him hadn't changed.

However, I was getting more than annoyed. So I asked why he was being so distant.

He said he's no good on his phone. He sent me love on socials. He was watching. But he was retreating. He was leaving me in slow motion. He told me he was flying back out for work and that seeing one another would be difficult because he has so much travel.

My heart sank.

How could I have wasted *months* on another guy?

Again…

I sent a voice message, asking he call this because I couldn't walk away. He needed to do it. I said I felt he was too nice to tell me things had changed.

Now, dear reader, I want you to pay attention to this because I need you to tell me if I missed something. Was I seeing something that wasn't there?

Nothing has changed!!! When we both have finished traveling, I'm sure we will make time to see each other. It's just bad. I'm horseshit on my phone. I want you to enjoy your trip. I also have travel coming up, and when we both come back, we will definitely catch up again.

You chase when I give you an out. Why?

He told me his schedule. It was clear I wasn't going to see him before he left. He would be gone for two months.

So what do you want to do? Do we put this on ice until you're back?

I will be 100 percent when I get back xx I fkn hate travel

So what do we do in the meantime? The time apart is a long time. A lot can happen. I've made clear what I want. Do you want to continue with how things are? X

Things are fine how they are xx

And that's how our story ends…

I wish there was more, but there isn't. As anticlimactic as those words are, they were the last spoken after months of building something I don't even know was real.

Things were clearly not fine.

He had time to see me. I asked…again if we could see one another before he left. We had a five-day holiday. He sent a picture with the caption, **Things are really busy at the moment, and I'm really sick.**

I didn't have any reason not to believe him, right? I mean, he was the one who reiterated endlessly that nothing had changed, and he was all in. But Dimples was a liar, which is ironic as I remember he once told me that he is extremely loyal and gets upset when those he cares about aren't loyal in return.

Mötley was over, and we were drinking and laughing just as we always do. We were talking about Dimples because remember, my friends are just as invested in my affairs as I am. That's what all good friends do.

I remember reading a quote saying your best friend will hate your ex more than you do, and that's nothing but the truth with my besties.

I replied and was left delivered for hours which sadly wasn't an uncommon occurrence of late, hence the confusion and many questions of, what the fuck?

He did say he was sick, so I figured he was resting. But social media is a blessing and a curse.

He posted a story.

It was a bottle of tequila.

And…it was a girl.

My heart sank.

I didn't want to jump to conclusions, but when he posted another video of them in the car, singing and dancing, I knew my feelings were warranted.

I knew things weren't okay, but he promised me they were.

But he also promised me so many times that he would see me.

Dimples was a liar.

And I soon came to learn he was a coward as well.

I tried not to speculate, but it's not hard to see where this is going. It took me less than five minutes to piece together what was going on.

The girl was someone new. My besties did the research and found her on his socials. He dropped the fuckboy go-to fire emoji on her post.

The next day, they both posted the same thing—early morning smoothies.

I don't need to draw a Venn diagram. We know where this is headed.

I think it's safe to assume they spent the night together if their early morning drinks were anything to go by. He wasn't being secretive about it, so I guess he didn't see an issue with what he was doing.

It cheapened everything we shared.

It felt as though I fabricated this entire thing between us.

If I had any doubts about his intentions with his new squeeze, he wrote publicly on her posts that she was so beautiful. Drooling and love eyes emojis in case she missed the memo. Funny, he said the same thing to me, emojis included.

He followed her best friend, and if I needed any more proof, he FINALLY opened my messages a day later and left me on read.

Yup, that's all I was worth to him.

After patiently waiting for someone who I thought was waiting for me, Dimples ended whatever we were with silence.

That hurt.

It hurts because today is the day that this happened. I'm sitting here writing as I always do to help deal with these feelings I don't understand. I don't understand when the shift happened. Or why, especially when he promised me that nothing had changed.

The day he told his new squeeze she was so beautiful was the same day he sent me those messages you just read.

How does one think it's okay to send something like that to one woman and say something to another?

It's not okay.

What Dimples did is not okay at all.

In a sense, I feel relief that I wasn't going crazy. That my gut feelings were, in fact, real. When I questioned Dimples, he would assure me things were okay. But they weren't. And that's why I kept asking him if he had lost interest because he had.

What I don't understand is why he never took the outs?

I gave him so many. Yet he stayed. He promised nothing had changed, and I believed him. I mean, why would he lie?

What did he have to gain by stringing me along?

I still don't know. And I don't think I ever will.

Telling a girl that she's beautiful and promising me on the same day we were Kosher is a deal-breaker for me. I do not intend to find out what went wrong because I wouldn't believe a word.

History proved time and time again that Dimples is nothing but a liar, but I chose to ignore the signs because I didn't understand why he would humor me for months if he didn't mean a word of what he said. What did he gain from it?

We saw one another twice.

That's all.

But our situationship lasted for months.

During that time, we got to know one another, and the distance apart didn't divide us. We both stuck through it, only for it to end like this.

I don't understand why he would put such an effort into "us." Because when he could have me, he didn't want me. But when he was away, he gave me the boyfriend experience.

Perhaps one day, I will get the answer I seek. But for now, Dimples doesn't deserve a second thought.

My cheerleaders have given me a reprieve, but the inevitable "I told you so" lingers. I always knew we came with an expiration date, but I honestly never foretold that it would end this way.

Perhaps, I pushed him away with my insecurities. But it seems they were warranted because he did exactly what I thought he would.

That first month, he was solid and legit. I honestly believe that. But the rest of the time, I don't know. I like to believe he meant everything he said, but once a liar, always a liar.

Maybe with age, Dimples will grow, but I honestly think he doesn't see anything wrong with what he's done. To post it publicly shows he has nothing to hide. That's a slap to the face, not going to lie. But you can't force someone to want to be with you.

Dimples didn't choose me. Neither did Ghost. Or Switzerland.

But I don't want to be a second thought. So if what they gave me was their best, I'd rather nothing.

And this is where I leave my story…for now, anyway.

So since the last line, there's been an update.

Dimples has reappeared.

Are we surprised?

No…

When I stopped caring is the moment he started. It seems to be this way for most things. I pulled my energy away, only for him to feel the shift and return tenfold.

But I was done.

My besties should work for the FBI because they did their digging in case I ever had a lapse in good sense again.

I haven't, thankfully.

But Dimples was quite the fuckboy, it appears, leaving a trail of broken hearts behind. But there was something which Mötley said and that was, he always comes back to you.

Why?

I have always been curious by nature, hence the shit I've found myself in.

He really tried to be genuine and sincere, confessing he has a hard time letting people in, and he didn't know why.

I listened, and I would be lying if I didn't admit I had a soft spot for Dimpleses. I don't know why because if this were happening to anyone else, I would have told them to delete his number months ago.

And that's why I wanted to include his chapter.

The more people I spoke to, the more I realized how many Dimples existed out there. Online dating honestly can be fucking insane and put you off dating forever, like forever forever.

You finally gather the courage to download the apps to see what the fuss is about, only to realize that they're full of fuckboys, grown men who *still* don't know what they want, or creeps. But when you finally find someone, you have hope that perhaps you found your unicorn, only to realize you've been catfished or you don't vibe in person.

Or better still, go on a few fantastic dates, only for you to be ghosted with no idea what went wrong.

But being the optimist, you continue with your search and settle, only to be ghosted for the ten billionth time. You've accepted you're never going to find your person there and uninstall the app, wanting to meet someone in the real world.

But to meet people in real life, you have to leave the house. And we all know what a horrible idea that is.

So you reinstall the apps a month later, hoping something has changed.

Nothing has…

It's tough, and when speaking to others, they can relate.

And this is why I wanted to write about Dimples.

Yes, I should have known better. And I know some will read this and say the same thing.

But this is such a common thing; a situationship gives you so much, and then gives you nothing but breadcrumbs to keep you hooked.

IYKYK.

I've been ghosted.

Been fooled into thinking that someone was the real deal.

And now, I was in a situationship with a fuckboy.

What could possibly happen next?

BROOKLYN

What could happen next is an expected turn of events.

But are we surprised?

No, we are not.

With his blue eyes, dark hair, ink, and smart mouth, I didn't stand a chance. And his name, his name is Brooklyn. He's from New York originally, and I met him on yet another app. You'd think I'd learn my lesson by now.

But nope, and you want to know why?

Insanity?

Glutton for punishment?

Yes, but the crux of it all is that I am a hopeless romantic and still want to believe in love.

I still like to believe that my Mr. Right is out there, regardless of all the Mr. Wrongs I've dated. I refuse to let bad luck, bad choices, break me because I am too stubborn for that. What I can say, however, is that these experiences have made me even more cautious and leaves the overthinker in me rocking in a corner and wishing this nightmare would be over soon.

I can honestly say that I wish I never met Brooklyn. He promised he was different…only to yell SURPRISE, I AM A LYING A-HOLE.

But let's take a trip down memory lane, shall we?

Like most events in my life, I was not looking for Brooklyn. Nor did I see him coming. He caught me completely unawares. I was in the US for work, and as one does, bored one night, I was scrolling through my matches and saw him.

By now, I'm sure you know what I like. That I look for that something, something, and Brooklyn had it.

Our original conversation was nothing spectacular. So much so that I forgot we had connected and left the US without giving him a second thought. A few days later, however, when I fell back into scrolling instead of writing, I saw that he had messaged, and I hadn't replied. I decided to rectify that, something I wish I hadn't because, well, you can guess why.

But as I always say, hindsight is fucking useless.

He seemed very upfront, and I liked his laid-back vibe. He was honest, and his communication was incredible. We added one another on socials and spoke incessantly every single day.

I woke to a good morning message. Only to send him a good night message back.

We made the time difference work.

Who said long distance doesn't work?

A wise mothertrucker, that's who.

During the weeks of us getting to know one another, we spoke nonstop for hours. The first time I called him, it honestly felt as though I had known him for years. There were no awkward silences or pauses. We spoke for about four hours, something which soon became our norm.

We literally spoke from sunrise to sunset, and it just felt…normal.

I never had this with the other men I was seeing. Yes, the past men and I talked a lot too, but I think I spoke more to Brooklyn than I conversed to my husband in the twelve years we were married.

Brooklyn made time for me and made me feel as though I was someone special.

He called when he needed to vent or needed advice. He called just to say hi. It was so incredibly refreshing because there were no games. Brooklyn made clear he liked me, and I liked him.

Our talk never really delved into the "heavy breathing, what are you wearing" kinda vibe. We discussed what we liked in the bedroom, and I was relieved to hear we were on the same page.

It was a match made in fuckery heaven.

Brooklyn and I got to know one another inside and out for weeks, and I honestly can say he is the first guy to ever do that. He *was* different.

I thought Ghost was a good communicator. But Brooklyn ran circles around any man I was with prior. But my heart was perpetually scarred due to being obliterated by men who promised they were different, only proving to be worse than their predecessors.

So I was wary.

I wanted to believe he was everything he said he was, but there was a catch.

There had to be.

So…I waited.

And waited.

But each day, Brooklyn was there, just how he said he was going to be.

My heart and brain were forever battling the other because this was unheard of, a man who actually was who he said he was.

My bestie and cosmic sister Mötley, who was by my side throughout every relationship, liked Brooklyn. She knew my ex-husband. She knew MR. J. She was there when I cried over Ghost. She had snacks and a bottle of wine in hand when Switzerland left.

It was she and I and *then* Dimples, as she often said, *we* had to remember he acted the way he did when things went wrong. It was never *you* have to remember; it was always *we*. And I love that regardless of her troubles, she always opened her heart to comfort me when I sank low.

She helped me wade through the tears to find my laughter again. We would play voice message ping-pong, consisting of nothing but laughter. The type of laughter where no sound comes out 'cause you're laughing so hard.

No one would understand the stuff we laughed about and that's the best kind of laughter. When just a look can trigger an onslaught of laughter where words are replaced with pure hysteria, that's the best kind of medicine for the soul.

I highly recommend it because laughter with my besties is what saved me from drowning in the sea of tears.

So it goes without saying, Mötley approving of Brooklyn had me falling deeper and deeper down the rabbit hole. He spoke to my friends, humoring them because they are my friends after all.

He edged his way into my world, and for once, I wasn't scared. I wasn't guessing if or when he would reply. I knew that he would because he proved himself time and time again.

When he didn't, he would apologize and explain why.

Once upon a married time, I had this. I had a man who made me feel safe. A man who delivered on his promises. A man who didn't play games. So I knew what it felt like. I knew what it felt like to like someone and have them like you back.

Brooklyn's messages soon became such a normal part of my days that we fell into this "situationship" without even really discussing it.

I made it no secret that moving to the US wasn't a pipeline dream. He asked where I wanted to move. I told him California. He was happy with my choice, and it was decided he would move with me.

Things were simple with Brooklyn, and after having complicated for the last…forever, it was a nice change.

He wasn't a romantic or a sweet talker. He was a realist. He was also extremely intelligent. He had a bit of a temper which I liked because he didn't take shit. He was old-fashioned in a lot of ways. But he also admitted he was a little brat.

He sent me a reel one day about people who get angry quickly. It really touched me because it detailed that beneath their fiery exterior was a soul filled with compassion that was quite sensitive to emotions. They feel both highs and lows intensely, so their anger is a protective shield. They love wholeheartedly. They invest so much emotion in their relationships that they can feel frustrated when they feel undervalued or overlooked.

I fell a little bit harder for him because no man had ever sent me something like that before.

Was he attempting to allude that this explained him? If so, I was hooked.

He didn't shy away from conversation and shared so much with me about his past.

The good.

The bad.

He told me everything.

We grew close.

As did my feelings.

I tried to stop them. But it was hard to defuse something that only continued to burn bright and be the light when you were lost in the darkness for so long.

Brooklyn was the surprise I did not see coming…but did I mention I fucking hate surprises?

Things were solid for a long time.

I knew his routine.

He knew mine.

We grew closer and closer, so it was inevitable that my original plans to stay for three days extended to six. He knew all along I was returning to America, so when the time came, I was both excited and nervous.

Before I boarded, he called, wishing me a safe flight.

When I landed, I had a missed call and a message from him.

I called him back, and it was surreal that we were finally talking in the same time zone. He expressed his excitement to see me. We had a week of work to get through before I would go down to see him.

It was a relief that things were still the same. That he didn't get cold feet. He was still the same man I had developed an attachment to.

But my guard was still up. History hasn't been kind to me and my heart. It had a photographic memory, and the pain associated with the memories was a reminder to be cautious because if something is too good to be true, then most times, it is.

But it's not all doom and gloom regarding my bad choices in love. My friends are to thank for that.

And cocktails.

My experiences with love have had me having some very interesting conversations as well as meeting some exceptional people. One of which I wrote about previously, and her name is Psychic.

Always putting my faith in the universe, I believe there is no such thing as coincidences, which is why when a year ago, I stumbled across a neon green palm reading sign in Times Square, I knew this was the universe speaking to me, and as I always say, when the universe speaks…listen.

And I am so glad that I did.

It was here I met Psychic.

Whether you're a believer or not, faith speaks to many in different ways, and for me, Psychic spoke to me when I needed guidance. She spoke to me during a time when no matter how many times I assured myself it would be okay, my heart wouldn't listen.

I fought against myself every day, and I was doubtful I would ever see the proverbial light at the end of the tunnel. The harder I tried to be "normal," the harder it got to breathe.

So when I stumbled across Psychic on that snowy night in New York, something inside me shifted, and I felt like me again. I wish I could explain it better. But sometimes there are no words to explain something that shouldn't make sense but does.

A year later, I walked the same street but with a different mind frame.

I felt "better."

Although I had experienced some really shitty things, I was a lot more centered. When I saw Psychic a year prior, I felt like a baby bird who had just learned how to fly. Now, I had taken flight and seen what was out there, and I needed her to undo something that continued to clip my wings.

Again, it doesn't make sense. But I couldn't help but feel that whatever Psychic had done with MR. J, I needed her to undo ASAP because I constantly felt as though my bad luck with men seemed to stem from that meeting.

It was as if MR. J was a huge roadblock, and whenever I made some sort of progress with men, something would happen and the last man standing was always MR. J.

Do we need a recap on who MR. J is?

My first love, the guy who broke my heart, only for me to go back a billion years later and for him to break it all over again.

Don't shake your head at me. I know what a dumbass I am.

Alas, me all but breaking down Psychic's door to help lift this voodoo love spell so I could find my Prince Charming and live happily ever after.

I suppose I did leave a huge part out of the story. Yes, I was coming to the US for work, but my pit stop was simply to undo the pact I made with the universe because she had made me bleed, and I was done.

I had mentioned to Brooklyn I was going to New York before seeing him. He had asked why. I was apprehensive at first to share why because what I was doing wasn't everyone's cup of tea. He began to worry, however, and asked if I was going there to see another man.

I liked there was a little possessiveness to his tone.

When I told him the reason, he simply laughed and said he wasn't a believer but was interested in hearing what she said.

I pressed the buzzer, and the glass door opened. When I climbed those familiar stairs, a sense of peace and calm settled over me.

I knew I made the right choice.

Pizza place on the lower level.

Tattoo studio on the second.

And on the third was Psychic's home.

I didn't even have a chance to knock on her door. She opened it and said, "You were supposed to call me."

I was supposed to do a lot of things…but here we are.

I *was* impressed that she remembered me. But she is psychic, after all. She went about spraying down my hands and shoes just like last time and then welcomed me into her home. Everything was the same. And again, that sense of peace wrapped me in a tight embrace.

I didn't regret this detour one bit.

I sat in the chair across from her, and she sighed. Could she sense the shit I was in?

Her silence made me nervous, so I blurted out, "I need you to undo whatever you did with Mr. J and I. Please."

She leaned back in her seat and looked at me with those knowledgeable eyes. "I warned you."

"I know, and I'm an idiot who didn't listen. Now please help."

She nodded, and I noticed when deep in thought, she rocked slightly, nodding. It's not unnerving. It's actually beyond fascinating to watch.

"I didn't do anything," she finally says.

"Um…"

"If you think I did some love spell or coercion, then you're mistaken. I don't make people fall in love. All I did was open you up to the universe. The rest is your fate."

I sat for a moment, unsure how I felt about what she had revealed.

For one year, I believed that whatever was done here, in this very room, was the cause of my bad luck with men.

Turns out I was wrong.

I didn't know whether to be disappointed or relieved. It was easy to believe that my luck was because of some voodoo love spell I signed in blood with the universe, but that wasn't the case.

My choices were the reason. Every action has a consequence, and this was mine.

And that also meant that what Mr. J felt was real.

Well, that was a plot twist I did *not* see coming.

Psychic read my disbelief and desperation and nodded. "Lean back and close your eyes."

I did as she asked.

She told me to go to my happy place.

That was easy—the beach.

Water has always calmed me, which is ironic because I can't swim. I've almost drowned twice. But regardless, I have always felt at peace near water.

So in my mind, I went to the beach.

I sat on the sand and peered out into the vastness and just…breathed.

"Open your eyes."

When I did, I felt…different.

Perhaps like a weight had been lifted from my chest. Whether this was my mind playing tricks or Psychic, in fact, undid whatever I forged with the universe, it didn't matter because I felt better. I was happy I did something, no matter how crazy to some, which made me happy.

And I am all about self-love these days.

Then Psychic asked me to say the name of the man I was interested in three times.

I did.

Brooklyn.

Brooklyn.

Brooklyn.

And I waited with bated breath.

"He's not for you."

Well, that was as anticlimactic as they come.

Psychic doesn't believe in sugarcoating anything, and that's okay. But I can't deny I felt my stomach drop in disappointment.

Look what happened the last time I didn't listen to her.

But a small part of me knew she was right.

Where had this traitorous part come from?

The moment I said his name, it felt wrong. I suddenly felt like a love impostor.

"You've not met him yet. Or been intimate."

Again, I need to reiterate, these are not questions she asked, but rather statements she made because she knew.

All I could do was nod.

For the next twenty minutes, she told me things that no one but the two people involved in the relationship should know. But Psychic summed up Brooklyn so accurately that I was gobsmacked.

She detailed that he wasn't very open about his past relationship, and that was because he got his heart broken. He had walls up.

This was starting to sound all too familiar.

She said he suffered from depression and anxiety, which he did.

"He uses you as a counselor."

"Yes. He calls when something is wrong, or he's anxious."

She raised a brow. "You do not want that in a partner. You need someone who will support you. You're not his mother. You've done enough of that in the past with partners. No more. Stop putting others before your own needs.

"It's bad energy transfer. They suck all they can from you before there's nothing left but a husk of who you once were."

I couldn't have said it better myself.

"You're moving to America. Have you met the older man with money?"

This was a lot to digest.

I just stared at her, mouth agape.

"I know you like men younger than you. You like the ones who are pretty on the outside. They know it, and they act on it."

Meaning they were usually fuckboys, or fuckboys with training wheels.

She was right.

But how do you stop something which you know is going to burn you, but you want to touch…so…damn…badly.

"Show me a photo of the younger one you like."

Dimples.

When I did, she shook her head once again. "He sleeps around. Please use protection with him. He likes you, but he is young. Don't expect much from him."

Which I already knew.

"Show me a picture of Brooklyn and Mr. J."

I did.

She sighed.

By this stage, I was pretty sure she wished I never stumbled across her sign at midnight. But I knew that wasn't the case.

I could see the compassion in her eyes, and all I could think was you won't heal by going back to what broke you.

I don't know where this came from. But the proverbial "epiphany" hit at that moment.

Whatever happened, I needed to remember the reason I left. The reason the men in my life were no longer an integral part of my narrative.

"Brooklyn is not in your future." She didn't elaborate, but I knew she meant business. "Mr. J…hmm…"

Hmm is never good.

"A blood tie binds you to him."

I had no idea what that meant.

"Soulmate, twin flame, these are good things. A blood tie is not."

No surprise there.

She went on to ask about his family history, and I was amazed when I answered yes to most things she queried about. She said our bond was strong, and sometimes, we're fated to the wrong people. But that doesn't mean they're bad.

It just means that sometimes, shit happens, and life doesn't work out the way you want.

I've learned to accept that.

But the tie I had with Mr. J, it did make me think that there is a reason we keep coming back to one another. I never wish to paint him in a bad light. He just didn't want what I did. Yes, he is frustrating, but one cannot condone him for feeling the way he does.

He never intentionally set out to hurt me. Unlike Ghost, who had a chance to make things right. But he chose to be a chickenshit about it. Mr. J just didn't want a relationship. How could I be mad at him for that?

We gravitated back to one another because our connection, our chemistry, wasn't the issue—it was all the other stuff in-between.

And now that Psychic mentioned some supernatural tie as such, I felt like he and I were always meant to be in each other's lives in one way or another.

I spent two hours with Psychic. She said some things that are too personal to share. I believed what she said because she just knew too much. She spoke about a trauma in my childhood that I only recently faced. She then spoke about my work and then the inevitable—the bad luck I have with men and why that is so.

We also spoke about my latest book. She congratulated me for being so vulnerable. She knew what it was like for people to look at you funny because you're one of the "weird" ones. We really connected.

We spoke like old friends, and in the end, she told me a lot about her past. Of how she came about to where she was.

Her mother was Bruce Springsteen's spiritual adviser. You can look this up. It's all true. She told me about her family history, and it read like a novel. I was so intrigued by her. I like to think that when we meet someone, we take a piece of knowledge away from that meeting; something that we didn't know, perhaps.

And with Psychic, I felt nothing but love and warmth from this exceptional woman.

I don't know why we met, but I'm so thankful for it.

She had another client, so it was time to say goodbye. But she asked me to come back tomorrow. Our time together wasn't done.

When I've told others this story, the first thing they'll say is how much did she charge? They instantly assume that Psychic was in it for the money. She wasn't. What she charged me is less than what I've spent on lunch.

She hugged me and promised that good things are ahead.

Those things, however, didn't include Brooklyn.

I went for a long walk after seeing Psychic. I needed to decompress. It was…a lot.

Brooklyn called. He wanted to know how things went with Psychic because although he wasn't a believer, it seemed curiosity got the better of him.

I couldn't stop thinking about what she had said about him. Were our days numbered? When would be the precise moment things turned?

I decided to leave out those details but told him the rest. I could hear he was impressed. He then asked where I was. I told him Central Park and that I was going to go for a run tomorrow morning.

He was horrified and concerned for my safety because it was dangerous to be running by myself in the dark. I was touched by his concern. He reiterated he didn't want me doing it because he was worried.

I swooned.

We spoke for hours as I explored. Although I have been to Central Park many times before, I always find something new. And I loved exploring Brooklyn's home ground while talking to him. Being with Brooklyn was effortless. There never was an uncomfortable silence. We always found something to talk about.

But in the back of my mind, Psychic's words played over and over. Not to believe her meant all the other things she had predicted were wrong.

I was so torn.

But what's new?

New York City is my spirit animal.

I'm convinced I lived here once upon a time. I never feel like a stranger when walking the streets, and I always find my way to where I want to go. To someone who gets lost regularly, this is something.

I caught up with friends.

I ate some really good food.

And I saw Psychic one last time.

She gave me a blessing and bid me good luck.

But we both knew this wouldn't be the last time we spoke.

Ironically, the same night I saw her, Dimples sent me a long-winded message, professing his undying "love" for me. It was reflective of all the other love bombs he had sent. But damn, he opened up and sent a thesis on his "feelings" for me.

I replied with a cordial thanks for being so open and left it at that. Our time had come and gone. But I did find it interesting that after weeks of radio silence, he sent me a message such as that.

I asked Psychic, and she said during her blessing, all she did was open me up to the universe. What will be, will be. So perhaps Dimples did mean everything he sent.

But it was all too little, too late.

Psychic hugged me one last time, and I felt nothing but kindness emanating from her heart.

"Call me any time. You have so much happiness waiting for you. The universe is ready."

But the question was, was I?

"Life is about luck. As well as chance. Numerology plays a big part in everything."

At this precise moment, I thought of my lucky numbers.

"Your lucky numbers are three and seven."

My mouth dropped open because they are indeed my lucky digits.

"How did you know *that*?" I stupidly asked.

Psychic looked at me like, *are you serious right now?*

Her parting words will stay with me always. "Because I'm psychic."

Silence…before I burst into laughter.

She smiled, shaking her head.

Seems that Psychic is my spirit animal too.

I left her studio with a happiness in my heart.

I believe that we meet every person for a reason. Whatever the reason, I'm still attempting to figure that out. But I never take a moment for granted because life is made up of beautiful snippets in time that make up your past.

And that had me thinking about what Psychic said about Brooklyn.

I put my faith in her, so to hear her say he wasn't in my future left me out of sorts. What she said about him didn't reflect the person he was. Of course I don't take every word she says as gospel, but she's been accurate about a lot of things.

I confided in Mötley about what she said.

Being the forever bright light in a withering storm, Mötley said perhaps it was because we hadn't met and our energies hadn't mixed yet. Which is what

Psychic said. She forever tries to see the positive in everything. Even when her world is shrouded in darkness, she always has time to calm my manic; being around her calms the chaos.

She reminded me that this was Brooklyn, the guy who had been nothing but honest, responsive, and reliable. He didn't play games. He was habitual in a way that I liked. She had read his messages. Heard his voice notes. She was as part of this "relationship" as I was.

She assured me that when we met, things would be fine because the connection we had was real.

She was right, but it's nice to hear it from a friend to confirm that what you're feeling isn't just made up in your head.

Brooklyn and I spoke like normal, and I pushed aside Psychic's words of warning.

But I really shouldn't have.

It was the day before I was flying out to another state for two days. Then after this, I was coming to see Brooklyn. It was a beautiful day in New York, and as always, I was walking the streets with no real place to go.

I was on the phone with Brooklyn, and he was telling me about his day like always. He asked when I was arriving again, and I jokingly commented that this was the tenth time I had told him.

Things took a turn.

He responded in a way that I didn't appreciate. He was rather abrupt, and his tone quite blunt. I ended the call and decided to take the night off from speaking to him.

The following morning, on the way to the airport, he texted me.

I guess you don't like me anymore.

I didn't want to make a big deal about this, which I sent back, and I just explained that I didn't like how he spoke to me.

He replied gruffly, saying he wasn't going to pretend he knew what I was talking about and that he didn't say anything disrespectful. I didn't have a chance to reply before he said if I felt disrespected for whatever reason, then maybe it's a good idea that we don't hang out.

My stomach dropped, and I instantly began doubting myself.

Had I overreacted?

Maybe I shouldn't have said anything?

But then, I remembered all the times I didn't say anything and how those relationships ended. No, I wasn't second-guessing my decision.

I replied that his tone wasn't appreciated, and I also never said I felt disrespected. But if he didn't want to hang out, then that's fine.

I wasn't going to beg for anyone's time because if you take anything away from this tale, it's this: we don't chase, we attract.

His attitude changed drastically.

He said he wasn't making fun of me and was only joking. That I had misunderstood, and he wasn't that type of person. But he said that I literally ghosted him last night, and he thought I was looking for an excuse not to talk to him anymore.

Reading these texts back, I can't help but see the irony in them—you'll soon see why.

He said that if I wanted to play games, he was not the guy for me. It was all a misunderstanding, and he wasn't being nasty. I would know if he was.

We made peace, but I couldn't help but feel that something had shifted. I saw a side to him I didn't like. I understand people have bad days and can be misunderstood, but Brooklyn's tone was mean. And I don't like mean people.

Things went back to normal, but something didn't sit right in the pit of my stomach, and we know what that is, right?

Gut instinct.

Never ignore it because it is rarely wrong.

The day had come.

I was a nervous bundle of excited energy.

I boarded the plane with no real expectations.

Frankie, a friend, was picking me up from the airport. We were spending the week together, as she lived not too far from Brooklyn. Our meeting at the airport was filled with hugs and smiles. Frankie is my girl. She knew about Brooklyn and was excited to meet him too.

I settled in and texted him.

He said he was running some errands but would come later. He also made clear that he wanted to stay the week if it was okay with Frankie, which of course it was.

It helped to have a friend there, but I realized it might be daunting for him, so I suggested we meet at the beach to ensure we didn't hate one another first.

Frankie and I caught up, and like always, it was like no time had passed since the last time we saw one another, which was over a year ago. Frankie's heart is so big and kind. I feel blessed to be in her presence because I love, admire, and respect her so much.

So her opinion of Brooklyn meant something to me.

We were drinking cocktails by the pool when Brooklyn called.

This was it.

The time had come…or not.

"My cat hasn't come back, so I can't come."

Okay, being an owner of three cats, I get this. I too would be a mess if they didn't come home when they're supposed to.

This wasn't an excuse, I assured myself, because I knew how much his cat meant to him. He loved all animals, which was one of the many things I liked about him.

I said it was okay and to come see me when it suited him.

We hung up, and I told Frankie and some other friends who had arrived, all of whom were like *what the fuck?*

Really?

His cat...

I couldn't help but feel that perhaps this was an excuse, after all, but I didn't want to believe that it was.

What will be, will be, and I enjoyed the night with my friends.

The following morning, Brooklyn texted.

He was definitely coming after work and staying.

And I believed him.

Frankie had the cure to my nerves—cocktails, of course.

Another friend was flying in to spend time with us. Pinkie.

Pinkie's heart is too big for this world. She is nothing but smiles and love. I can tell her anything and know she will listen for as long as I need to vent. And vice versa because she has the best stories. She offers the best advice, and being in her presence just makes me so happy. There is a warmth about her that is so contagious.

I told her about Brooklyn and the other boys I had tragic romances with. It was nice to catch up. Through thick and thin, my friendships are forever present, reminding me that no matter what happens, those relationships are real.

A few cocktails in, Brooklyn called and said he would be at the house in an hour.

It was happening—like really happening.

And us three friends did what any good friends would do—we frantically moved my things to the third floor. I think back on this with such fondness.

It was a flurry of excitement as we giggled about all the things friends giggle about.

My friends carried all my things, thrilled that I could potentially meet "the one."

They knew about the non-ones, so they were rooting for me.

We made the bed in the prettiest linens and I threw a bunch of clothes at them, asking for their opinion on which they liked best. This also applied to lingerie and sleepwear.

Nothing is off-limits when it comes to my friends.

With everything settled, I showered and got ready.

Brooklyn texted and said he was ten minutes away. Okay, now I was just damn nervous.

I texted Mötley, who, as always, made me feel better. She wanted hourly updates, regardless of the time difference.

Talking to her always calms me.

I could do this.

If we didn't vibe, then we didn't. I was happy I was courageous enough to put myself out there because you've read my tragic past.

Frankie waited for Brooklyn in the driveway, sipping her cocktail; god, I love that woman.

His truck pulled in, and I died.

This was it…there's no turning back now.

I waited by the pool as Frankie greeted him. I could see by her face that she approved. The time had come.

It's all a little surreal, and no matter how many positive affirmations you recite, nothing really prepares you for this.

Brooklyn was moving his truck, and Frankie ran over, saying he was cuter than his pictures and it was really him. I wasn't being catfished. He was taller than I thought, and he was nervous.

I got the rundown in ten seconds.

That's all I needed to hear.

I waited for him, and the moment he stepped from his truck, the first thing I noticed was how blue his eyes were.

And yes, he was taller than I thought.

He said hello in that deep New York accent that had become my soundtrack for weeks, and then he kissed me.

Did I feel the proverbial butterflies?

Was it love at first sight?

No.

Not the answer I was expecting either. But I had that with men prior, and we all know how those ended.

So I didn't read too much into it because when we hugged, it warmed every part of me from head to toe. And that, to me, is just as important as feeling that spark when you first kiss.

Brooklyn met my friends and was very polite.

I watched him engage and liked that he held eye contact and was confident but not arrogant. He held his own and was the alpha he claimed to be.

I could see he was exhausted from work, so we went upstairs. The entire time, I was waiting for that something, something. The cute-meet moment.

But it never came.

It was just…weird.

I don't know what I was expecting, but I guess because we had spoken for so long, I thought we might bypass any weirdness.

But something was missing.

He made some calls for work, and I sat across from him, watching him.

This was the guy who had tackled me out of nowhere and made me feel things I didn't want to experience again. And now that he was here, my head and my heart battled.

My head screamed at me to listen to my gut, but my heart only wished to remember all the beautiful things we shared.

Yes, he was gorgeous, but I learned that looks are the most minuscule part of liking someone. Looks faded, but the connection didn't, and I wasn't feeling it.

I scolded myself for being so negative. I always try to be positive and see the best in every circumstance.

I could see he was nervous. The silence was also noticeable by him.

"Are you mad at me?" he asked, which caught me off guard.

"Of course I'm not."

He was becoming frustrated with something not going his way, and his anxiety kicked in.

I sat by him and gave him a hug.

Hardly how I envisioned our first meeting going, but throughout my life, I have come to learn not to expect anything as this stops one from being disappointed. A bleak way to view things and people, but it's a realistic slap to stop me from getting my heart broken—again.

We went into the bedroom and decided to watch some TV.

This is always an awkward moment for me, and it seemed like it was for Brooklyn too because we lay as far away from one another as possible. I was so far on the edge, I may as well have been back in Australia.

But as the sun surrendered to the moon, Brooklyn moved closer and closer.

I liked the way he smelled. A mixture of bubble gum and something else I couldn't quite distinguish. His natural scent, perhaps.

When he grabbed me by the waist and dragged me toward him, I finally felt it.

That something, something. But it was diluted. I ignored it when I shouldn't have.

He kissed me; soft at first.

But I didn't travel halfway across the world for soft.

So I did what I said I would; I pulled his hair and kissed him hard.

And then it was game on.

We made out for a very long time, familiarizing ourselves with the other.

This is one of my favorite moments with the guy I like.

It's new and exciting, and the promise of this turning into something more fills my heart with faith.

Things got hot and heavy, and my body liked everything Brooklyn had to give. The passion was there, but was it like with Switzerland or Dimples?

No.

It definitely didn't hold a candle to Ghost.

But I took that as a good thing because where had those relationships left me?

Crying for weeks, that's where.

We didn't have sex because Brooklyn didn't bring any condoms. I liked that he hadn't assumed. Or that he hadn't had them on hand. We were on the same page when it came to safe sex.

He also realized he left his boots and medication at home.

He asked if it was okay if he didn't stay over as originally planned.

I said of course. I don't want anyone doing something they don't want to do.

He kissed me on the forehead and left.

Two nights had passed, and Brooklyn wasn't in my bed.

Did I think it was a little sus?

Yes, I sure did.

Mötley, once again my saving grace, counseled me from the other side of the world, but we both knew something wasn't right.

The next day, Brooklyn assured me he was staying over.

His bags were packed.

My friends told me they liked him. They thought he was polite and keen on me. He didn't shy away from answering their questions and was more than open and honest.

He was who he said he was.

I was happy, but there was this niggling little feeling in the pit of my stomach. I wished it would go away, but it didn't.

Brooklyn came over after work, and he looked gorgeous. He kissed me hello, and it amazed me that it felt so normal.

So what was the issue, then?

We spent the night with my friends who approved more so than ever. He was making an impression on them. And on me too.

So when we went upstairs, the inevitable was looming.

This was it.

Clothes were thrown off in haste, and when the moment came, the sex was…okay.

Was it earth-shattering?

No.

Was I disappointed?

Yes.

Sex is important in any relationship and I just wasn't feeling it.

This was bad.

This was so bad that I couldn't remember the last time I had sex that was this lukewarm.

How could this happen? Things were so hot between us on the phone. But in person, I may as well have been freezing my ass off in the North Pole because that's how fucking cold things were between us.

But that didn't sway my feelings because I couldn't deny that I liked Brooklyn.

And he told me he felt the same.

But was that enough?

It was the first night he slept over.

In some ways, I wish he hadn't because sharing a bed with a new partner should be exciting. But in the middle of the night, I awoke to rustling.

Had a mouse snuck into the room?

The mouse was in fact Brooklyn eating Reese's Butter Cups like he was preparing for a zombie apocalypse.

I got the ick.

This early on…this wasn't good.

He then slurped his McDonald's soda.

Surely, this was done.

Nope.

More rustling.

More eating.

More slurping.

There is no coming back from the ick…

I woke up to his alarm.

He wished me a good day and said that he would see me later.

The ick has subsided a little, but when I saw the empty candy and chocolate wrappers thrown around the room like confetti, it returned because the little bish never goes once the ick has been had.

I told Frankie the deets as friends do, and she was happy for me. But she could see I wasn't goo goo gaga over this man.

He came over for dinner, and again, it was comfortable and relaxed.

He stayed again that night.

I was terrified of what loomed.

Please, for the love of god, please do not let it be a repeat of the previous evening.

We had sex, and it was a little better than the night before. But the ick was sitting on the sidelines, eating popcorn and shaking her head.

Was he the alpha he said he was?

No.

Did he live up to talks of his big game?

No.

But again, it didn't matter because I enjoyed our time together.

And so did he.

He texted me that day to tell me that in case I didn't know. I liked that he reassured me, as he knew what an overthinker I am.

He laid a kiss on my forehead that morning he left and told me he'd miss me.

That was the last night he would stay.

It was my last night before I left for another state.

I expected Brooklyn would stay.

So did Frankie.

As did my friends back home.

So when he called and said he wasn't staying, I felt like I had missed the memo.

When I asked why, he said his back hurt because of the bed, and I could understand why. But when he added that he needed to mow his lawn, I thought that was a euphemism for something other than cutting his grass.

But I felt rather stupid when I realized this wasn't an analogy for him being married or that I wasn't lost in translation.

It was my last night, and he wasn't going to spend it with me.

Frankie was just as confused as I was. She had seen us together. She said if he didn't stay the nights prior, then okay, but to decide not to stay on my last night was fucking pathetic. Another reason I love her; she tells it as it is.

I couldn't agree more.

Brooklyn, always the conundrum, said he'd come over after work because he still wanted to see me, regardless of him not staying.

He came over, and again, that weirdness between us lingered.

I didn't know why it was there. I didn't understand it. We got along so well on the phone, but in person, we were strangers.

We spent a few hours together.

I realized sex wasn't a motivator for Brooklyn, and it wasn't for me either.

He spoke about work and didn't really ask anything about the rest of my trip. It was then I remembered what Psychic had said.

"They suck all they can from you before there's nothing left but a husk of who you once were."

I realized that the conversations we had were very one-sided. When I spoke up or didn't agree with something, we didn't get along as well as I thought we did.

How did I miss this?

And when he said he needed to go home and cut his grass, I realized that I was actually okay with him not staying.

I walked him to the door, and he kissed me goodbye and said he would take me to the airport tomorrow.

I waved goodbye…and that was the last time I ever saw him.

Frankie listened to me ramble on about him and agreed his excuse was pathetic. I felt it was pointless him taking me to the airport. He should be here, and he wasn't.

I was sticking to my guns of not allowing another man to walk all over me.

He texted me an hour later, apologizing for not staying. This showed me that he was aware of his choices. I was honest and said I was disappointed he didn't stay.

Silence…

I didn't receive a reply until later in the morning I was leaving.

He said it should have counted for something that he came over after work.

I told him that it did, but I wasn't coming back for a very long time. Yes, I came to see Frankie too, but he was a big reason I flew here.

We exchanged messages back and forth. Neither of us backed down. He said he didn't mean to hurt my feelings and that he had a lot going on. He then said something that kicked me in the guts.

You were fun to hang out with, but it sucks you don't live here.

Fun? *Really?*

My response went along the lines of: *I was here all week, which is why I wanted to spend ample time with you to see if we vibed. If so, I would have come back sooner rather than later. I want someone who wants to be with me as much as I want to be with them. Telling me I'm fun to hang out with isn't an incentive for me to come back.*

I wasn't going to do this again.

His reply was heartfelt and like the Brooklyn I thought I knew.

He said he understood where I was coming from and apologized for making it seem he didn't want to spend time with me. He enjoyed our time together, and it was nice meeting my friends.

He then added I deserve somebody who wants to spend time with me, which wasn't the case with him. He was just mentally exhausted and didn't handle stress well. He wished me a safe trip.

And that was it.

He assured me we could still talk, but it just equated to silence.

Two days passed, and he decided to text me back. His message was curt and blunt, reminiscent of our phone call.

Was that a sign I should have paid attention to?

He said he wasn't ignoring me. He had a lot of things "popping off" the last two days and needed a break from his phone to decompress, and I've literally been complaining to him for days. And needless to say, he couldn't deal with that at the moment.

Well, fuck him too.

I had asked him what was going on as I didn't understand his silence. I wasn't complaining. I simply asked why the silence. His whole "I needed to decompress" was a load of shit because he was posting on his socials a lot, something which he rarely did, so his excuse of staying off his phone was total bullshit.

I answered the only way I could.

With silence because silence speaks volumes.

He texted me a few days later, which I really appreciated.

I just wanted to apologize for how I responded and acted the other day. You didn't deserve that, and I'm sure you probably aren't happy with me, and I respect that, but I just wanted you to know that I think you're a really wonderful woman, and I enjoyed chilling with you. I'm sure you've felt like I was ignoring you, and I should have texted you back. I was just really angry. I found out I owe a lot of money on some stupid things, so yeah, hope you've made it home safely.

My heart felt better because I felt the void of not speaking. To go from speaking every day to nothing was hard, cold turkey in a sense.

I was upset he didn't even check to see if I arrived home safely when I landed. But regardless, he texted me, so I felt that perhaps we could move on.

We exchanged a few messages, but the vibe was off, and the inevitable loomed.

He wasn't feeling it anymore, and I honestly just went into self-preservation mode again.

I had been home for about a week and thought I would try one last time.

Good morning. I miss you in my bed.

It took him a day to reply.

Aw sorry I thought I replied to this. I hate this. All texted out.

And that was the last thing he ever said to me, that he was all texted out.

I didn't reply, torn with what an appropriate response would even be.

I decided to be honest. It was a short message.

Hi. Miss you. Hope you're okay x

Silence to the text, but he posted to his stories that good times make weak men and hard times make tough men or something like that.

The next day was my final attempt to salvage something dead and buried.

Is everything okay? Going from talking every day to not knowing if you're going to reply or not really messes with my head. If you don't wanna talk anymore, I respect that. Just let me know. I hope you're okay x

And that's where our story ends.

Brooklyn ghosted me.

He didn't reply.

He didn't unfriend or block me, but he hasn't made any contact either.

I can read between the lines because sadly, this has happened before. And because of that, I began to think that perhaps it wasn't the men I chose, but rather, perhaps the issue was me.

Those familiar feelings of not being good enough for anyone rose like wildfire, and I couldn't breathe. There was a common denominator, and that was me.

Bossman's words echoed loudly: *You had to go and create drama because you thrive on it. You self-sabotage your happiness because nothing is ever good enough for you!*

I questioned myself, just how I did when he said those words to me.

Maybe he was, god forbid, right.

But I didn't think I did that. I wanted simple. All I wanted was to find my person. How could it be this hard?

I know anything in life that is worth doing isn't easy, I've accepted that and am not afraid of hard work. But finding my person was bordering on being impossible.

What was wrong with me? Am I the problem here?

I asked my besties Mötley and Angel this very question. Regardless of my actions, my friends would always have my back. But I wanted—I needed—honesty because I just didn't understand what I was doing "wrong."

But what they said helped heal my soul.

We've read the messages, we've heard the voice notes and calls, so these men fooled us too. We believed, like you did, they meant everything they said to you. We've read your replies. You are not the problem here because if you are, then so are we.

Perhaps we're as delirious as the other, but it made me feel better.

We're so quick to judge others.

They're abundant in life.

Successful. Social.

Pretty.

They must have it all.

But we don't know anyone's struggles. Regardless of what one might portray on the outside, every person has their own struggles and demons.

And mine threatened to choke me, and for good this time.

Writing has always been an escapism for me, and I never take it for granted. I know what an extraordinary life I live, and I have every single one of you who is reading this to thank for that.

When I write, I leave pieces of myself throughout the pages, hoping to connect with you in some way. That is the reason I wrote this book.

LOVE HARD was an introduction, but LOVE HARDER is just that…if you're here for the second round, then it seems I was able to connect with you in some way.

Love isn't easy, and most times, it hurts, but we're still here, and that counts for something, right?

This was my mind frame when trying to deal with yet another heartbreak.

I tried not to let yet another failed attempt at love get me down, but it was fucking hard.

Brooklyn was supposed to be different, and again, I felt so incredibly stupid for believing in "love."

So for me, when trauma occurs, I can either write or I can't. And for months after my divorce, I couldn't write a single word. I was terrified I was about to face the same fate.

But alas, besties, what you hold in your hands is what happens when someone's heart gets broken. Words saved me, and perhaps, I wrote this for me. I wanted to print it to look back on a time in my life when I wanted to give up, but I didn't.

And I hope LOVE HARDER can provide the same comfort for you.

Never give up because life is full of lessons, good and bad. Just remember, those scars we all have, we're braver than what tried to break us.

Be fucking proud.

So, Brooklyn, I thank you for being a chapter I didn't see coming. Thanks for the memories…regardless of the fact you did what you promised you said you'd never do.

Now, let me revisit what I just said because something incredible has happened... *But alas, besties, what you hold in your hands is what happens when someone's heart gets broken. But it's also what happens when someone's heart gets healed.*

THE UNICORN

Life likes to throw me plot twists too, dear reader, because this chapter was unplanned. I accepted the four men you've just read about as a lesson learned and slapped a "do not resuscitate" on these "relationships" because these men were dead to me.

But it appears the best was yet to come. And I mean that in every literal way.

And that's what brings us to man number five.

Surprised?

Yes, me too.

You've read my history with love. Some love affairs I wish I could forget. Others, a learning curve that taught me so much.

I never gave up on finding love. But I was beginning to think this crazy little thing called love was nothing but fiction.

But perhaps that was because…I was just looking in all the wrong places.

The Unicorn was able to achieve in less than twenty-four hours what my husband could not in ten years.

Don't be looking at me with those judgy eyes.

I'm not just talking sexually because we all know that is a minuscule part of what I look for.

He seemed to have that something, something, and then some…I was so fucking screwed.

Life has a funny way of yelling SURPRISE, expecting you to keep up when you're driving blind. Like all monumental moments in life, he entered my world when I least expected it.

Writing about him will prove to be the hardest thing I've ever written. How will I ever find the right words to express my feelings for the man who changed my world? No words will ever be enough.

He was my type which always equates to trouble and tears.

But he impressed me from the get-go.

I don't know why or how.

I never do.

He had that something, something that I look for and the past has proven that that something, something always ends in a little something called heartache.

We matched.

He asked to call.

We spoke for hours, and then he stood at my door in less than twenty-four hours.

All my friends knew this was so common for me—living spontaneously, as it was with him. They said this was either the best or worst idea I've ever had, which is why I had no expectations.

I never do—I avoid disappointment this way.

Look at the previous men in my life. I got to know them because that's the "sensible" thing to do. Ensuring that your potential beau won't cut you up into tiny pieces and dance in front of a mirror wearing your skin as a meat suit.

But I did that, and it still ended horribly.

So after speaking to Mötley, I decided why the hell not? She said do it—he's been brought to you for a reason. The universe never lies.

What's the worst that could happen?

Probably not the best thing to think, considering I've never met this man and my clusterfuck history with the opposite sex.

But hey, *que será, será.*

And I was sick of overthinking.

This was the first time things felt right and fell into place.

There was never an uncomfortable pause on the phone, and we spoke for a very long time. It was unheard of because anyone who knows me, knows I would rather liaise via pigeon post than talk on the phone.

But things from the get-go always felt natural with him. He was witty, smart, and incredibly honest. And his voice gave me a tingle of the good kind.

I was skeptical, of course. I mean, what's the catch?

There's always a catch.

He was tall, dark hair, light eyes, tattoos…can we see where this is heading?

My "type" had done nothing but leave me wanting to rock in a corner and wishing I could erase every memory made of them.

But this was the last one, I promised myself.

No more.

If this went belly-up, then your narrator was giving up. Defeat is a dirty word, but my heart just couldn't take it anymore.

With that stance firmly in mind, I look back now and laugh because I was about to be thrown from the heavens with no safety net in sight.

Was I ready for the fall?

Hell to the fuck no.

He sent me a good morning message.

We all love that.

It's nice to know that someone is thinking of you when they first wake up, as opposed to messaging late at night because we all know how that scenario ends. I was still taken aback at how long we had spoken the night prior. I mean, this wasn't normal, right? A man asking to call to just…talk.

Shock.

Horror.

I was waiting for the catch; the entire time, I was waiting for The Unicorn to drop some bombshell so I could slap a DNF on him and shelve him with his fellow humankind. But as the day progressed, it seemed The Unicorn was sticking to his word, and after only twelve hours of "meeting," this date was, in fact, happening.

I was skeptical but humored the universe nonetheless.

The Unicorn was a gentleman; I sensed that from the get-go. He was old-fashioned in a sense as he wanted to go out for dinner. He lived a little while away from me and didn't assume he was staying the night. I gave him the address of where to meet, but he said he was hoping to come to my house prior and then we go out together. If this were any other guy, I would have guessed this was just a ploy to come over and no dinner would be had.

But not with The Unicorn.

I sensed he meant it.

Perhaps it was to see if we vibed, and if we didn't, then we could avoid an uncomfortable dinner where we'd be eyeing off the closest exit. But my gut was telling me he was doing this because he wasn't a fuckboy and that perhaps he could sense that something, something too.

I was running late as usual, so Mötley was taking one for the team and stepping in while I frantically got ready. I wasn't nervous. I never usually am when I meet someone new. Usually, the reason for that is because I've spoken to said person for at least a week prior to meeting. But with The Unicorn, I suppose in the beginning, I was more curious than anything.

Why had he captured my attention like no one had ever before?

When there was a knock on the door, those butterflies appeared, but I reminded myself that it is usually your good sense leaving your body. This was going to be yet another disappointment, one which I could learn from, and seeing as this was "the last time," I quashed down any expectations and went to meet the boy who drove close to two hours to see me.

However, before I had a chance to call it a night, Mötley tackled me in the hallway with a huge grin, nodding like a bobblehead. "You're going to like him. He is so FUCKING hot!"

Bless her potty mouth.

I felt remotely better because if she approved, then I knew I would too. But scroll back and reread what I said in regard to looks. They are the first thing that attracts most people to someone else, but I know if we're going to have chemistry from the first moment we meet.

And that is foolproof.

The Unicorn had bought an outfit and shoes (swoon) for our date and wanted to shower beforehand.

He was waiting for me in the kitchen, and when I entered…I knew I was in so much fucking trouble.

He was tall. Like really, really tall.

He was built how I like my men.

His eyes were the most beautiful color, but his smile…his smile was nothing but trouble in all the best of ways. I knew without a doubt, then and there, that The Unicorn was someone different.

Different how, I was still unsure of. But what I was sure of was that the universe was holding back, dropping losers in my lap to set the path for this man who killed me slowly with that smile.

I hated him already.

But behind that smile, he was guarded, and when I looked too close, he would peer at me with a look I would soon become accustomed to before he would wink. I don't know why, but I found the gesture leaving me with more questions than answers. But I also found it endearing.

The Unicorn was a Rubik's Cube, and just when I thought I had him figured out, I would turn a side, only to be faced with another avenue that would make him, him. Early on, he told me he was a walking red flag.

Was it a deterrent?

No fucking way.

Was he going to leave me guessing?

Hell to the fuck yes he was.

So with that in mind, I decided to see what the night held for us because I literally had started speaking to him just shy of twenty-four hours ago.

The moment Mötley left, and we were alone, I took a good look at my date for the night and liked every single thing he was throwing down. I wanted him to have a good night, so it was decided early on that neither of us would drive.

As we walked to the door, he grabbed me by the arm, turned me toward him, and kissed me.

This was the test.

Did I feel it?

The proverbial stars?

The butterflies?

The something, something?

Yes, I did.

It pulsated throughout my entire body.

The chemistry was there.

He kissed me how I liked.

He didn't shy away from showing me that he was the one in control, which I loved.

Although I am the dominant in my world, when it comes to the bedroom, I want my Superman to throw me around and pull my hair while whispering the dirtiest of things into my ear.

And The Unicorn delivered.

He gave me lots of eye contact, and when he slipped his hand under my dress, I knew I may have bitten off more than I can chew with this boy.

But I wasn't afraid.

I didn't feel objectified.

Or that dinner was a ploy.

On the contrary.

I felt as though I had met my match in every way.

Instantly, I noticed he opened the door, waiting for me to get in before him.

I liked that—a lot.

He was a gentleman, but what he did to me during the car ride revealed he also had no qualms taking charge. The Unicorn's hand remained under my dress. Again, the eye contact. And again, him revealing what a bossy, unapologetic man he was while I had to bite my lip to stifle what he was doing to me.

Though he wouldn't have done it if I didn't want it because I recognized The Unicorn as being quite observant. And this was cemented as the night progressed.

Once we arrived at the restaurant, which he was fine with me choosing, he opened the door again and held my hand as we walked the street. I couldn't help but think those incredible fingers were inside me moments ago.

Oh, the scandal…

We walked into the venue, a place that embodied the devil quite literally, which seemed fitting because I knew that once the night came to an end, I was going to be fucked into hell and back by this man who was setting me on fire as each second passed.

We sat down to dinner, and once again, the conversation wasn't forced.

There were no uncomfortable silences.

Or pauses.

There was never a moment when we weren't talking.

And I wasn't even drunk yet.

He didn't hold back and told me everything.

He was a father of three, something he was very proud of.

Another thing I liked about him—you can tell a lot about a man by the way he treats his children. And it was evident his kids meant the world to him.

He was quite young when he got together with his ex-partner, who was older than him.

It felt like he matured early.

Perhaps that's why I didn't feel him to be substantially younger than me because he was.

He went on to detail his past.

Was it rainbows and butterflies?

No, it wasn't.

But whose was?

Look at my clusterfuck history.

He didn't hold back.

He told me everything, and my country boy was a little bit of a bad boy at heart.

Did he flaunt it?

Wear it as some ridiculous badge of honor?

No.

He shared his past with me because he was honest, something which I detected early on.

I listened intently because he came from quite a large family, something which I always wanted. So I loved hearing his stories.

Mischief was something that seemed to follow.

I liked The Unicorn all the more.

We spent a few hours at dinner before we decided to go to a bar.

Love ♡ HardER

I've not made it a secret that I pay attention to detail, to the things most would overlook. But before I left, I needed to use the bathroom.

The Unicorn waited for me in the foyer, and when I exited, he peered up from his phone, did a second take, and gave me those sexy eyes boys give when they want to bend you over and smack your ass. He gave a cheeky soft catcall whistle before I slipped my hand into his.

Be still my heart...

He pulled me into his side, and we exited, still hand in hand.

Everything felt so natural.

It honestly felt like our tenth date.

Not first.

Again, he opened the door for me, and when we sat in the back, I took off a bracelet that holds meaning to me. I slipped it onto his wrist. He looked down at it and smiled.

He didn't ask why I had done it.

He just smiled.

And this is reflective of his favorite word.

"Sure."

I'd ask a question, and when he replied with the infamous "sure," I knew he was letting me do my thing as he wanted to please. It wasn't worth arguing over if he perhaps didn't want to do something unless strongly opposed or didn't agree.

It seemed he was happy just to allow me to lead.

He didn't want drama. Or for the night to be soiled.

He wanted easy.

As did I.

What a clever young man.

We got to the bar, and by this stage, your beloved pocket rocket of a narrator was rather drunk. We got our drinks and went to the outdoor area.

The Unicorn looked good.

He turned heads, which I liked as there is nothing more attractive than watching others want what you have, and I had The Unicorn.

Not once did I see him looking at other girls.

The only person he was looking at was me.

Our height difference was quite vast. I can imagine that is more than enough to have people look our way, but Mötley said there is an undeniable spark between us, which is more than addictive. People want in on whatever magic was brewing between The Unicorn and me.

I sat down, and like expected, the dogs came running.

This one was from Dublin.

The Unicorn sat on one side.

Dublin on the other.

Instantly, Dublin went in for the kill, whispering sweet nothings into my ear. I found it all rather amusing and decided to listen to his pitch. He was tenacious, I'll give him that. He laid on the charm, but it didn't matter what he said or did. The only man who captured my attention was The Unicorn. He sat silently, not needing to puff out his chest or whip out his dick to reveal who the bigger man was.

There was no pissing contest.

No staking his claim.

And that's because there was no competition.

The Unicorn simply exuded confidence, and that within itself was addictive.

Everyone wanted a piece of this man who was impressing me with each passing second. The air was rich with his dominant energy, and I quickly became addicted to the taste. Nothing is hotter than a man who knows what he wants and doesn't play games. A man who sits back and watches another man try to woo his date because he is that confident in himself.

"He can't handle a woman like you."

"He lacks confidence."

These were a few of the comments Dublin made, all of which I found rather entertaining as they were so far from the truth.

The Unicorn placed his hand on my thigh.

I felt that simple touch throughout my entire body.

Dublin continued his sales pitch for a little longer but gave up when he realized he could never compete with someone like The Unicorn, especially when I turned toward my date, and we kissed. It was established early on that The Unicorn and I like to share the same kind of kisses.

You can tell a lot from a kiss.

A little like *Goldilocks and the Three Bears*, but instead of beds…

This kiss is too hard.

This kiss is too soft.

This kiss is just right.

And the kisses between The Unicorn and I were just right.

He kissed me with passion and did that thing I like with his tongue. But you can tell a lot about someone by the way they kiss. I can say that now because The Unicorn and I have shared endless kisses since that night, so I compare them to now. At first, his kisses were passion-filled but missing something. Missing that intimacy because The Unicorn was guarded.

Walls were firmly in place and although he shared so much with me, he only let me see the superficial layers because perhaps The Unicorn was hurt by love too. I have a common theme when it comes to men; *LOVE HARD* delves into the depths of what.

I tend to fall for men who I want to be fixed.

The Unicorn didn't want me to fix him, so I knew he would be a tough egg to crack.

What was happening with The Unicorn had never happened before. To find that fire in all avenues is rare—not just looks, but personality and banter as well. After knowing one another for just a day, this was fucking unheard of.

I was constantly waiting for the other shoe to drop. I guess I still am.

Something this good to be true has to be, right?

The Unicorn's air of *whatever the fuck it is* drew fellow travelers to our table, and his ability to talk to those and make them feel welcomed was something that once again made him stand out from the rest.

I watched him closely because people watching is my thing. The way he held himself so confidently but without arrogance drew me in further. He didn't fill in the silence with small talk. He listened and engaged when he wanted.

He wasn't a people pleaser.

He radiated such intoxicating energy, it was almost suffocating. Being in his presence left me heady and almost out of breath.

We stayed at the bar for a while, chatting to people who asked how long we had been together.

I was honest and told them we had just met. This was greeted with laughter as no one seemed to believe it. Perhaps they too could feel the palpable chemistry between us, chemistry which was only continuing to grow.

I liked all the small things he did.

He pulled down my dress when it rode up a little too high before I had a chance to.

He would buy me a drink without asking.

He would watch where I would go if I decided to venture a little ways away.

This man was killing me, smalls.

Our next stop on the agenda was a club where there were no rules, no norm.

Everything goes.

It's my kind of place.

The Unicorn held my hand, taking it all in. This was so out of his element, but he didn't complain. He didn't make up some excuse that he left the stove on and had to go home. He took it all in and did what he does best; he observed.

As did I.

The Unicorn's sense of adventure appealed to me instantly.

He wasn't afraid to try new things.

Hell, he agreed to go on a date with an author he knew nothing about.

But it seemed he was up for almost anything.

A girl came over, and he gave her a twirl. All her Christmases had come at once.

Shock, horror, I am very possessive and have never been one to share my toys.

Was I jealous that some girl came over and tried to muscle in on my date?

No, I was not.

Did I want to push her down the stairs accidentally on purpose?

Perhaps.

The Unicorn read my reaction instantly and asked if I was jealous.

I said no.

He laughed, pulled me into his huge chest, and demanded I look at him as he rebuked my claims.

"You are so jealous," he said with a playful smile.

He was so enjoying this.

Maybe I was a little jealous? But I had forgotten what that felt like because, to be jealous, you actually had to care.

And I hadn't done that in a very long time.

He kissed me, and I wanted to eat him alive.

A primitive response, perhaps because we're all just animals in the end, and out here in the wild, I needed to stake my claim on The Unicorn.

But it was getting late, and like Cinderella, I was about to turn into a pumpkin as it was well after midnight. The Unicorn, however, wasn't ready to call it a night.

I was more than happy for him to go out without me since I needed sleep. And I am not one of those people who needs to tag along 'cause of FOMO. When I am done, I am done.

But The Unicorn said something to me that cemented my fate.

"That's not how it works," he said, engulfing me in his huge arms, ensuring I looked at him as he continued. "We go together. We leave together."

Where the fuck had this man come from?

I could question that tomorrow because he stuck true to his word. If I wanted to leave, he was coming with me. We caught a ride home where, in that back seat, he once again unapologetically made me squirm. He never broke eye contact; all I could do was succumb to the most beautiful deviant I had ever met.

My body responded to him in ways that had never happened before. It usually takes a lot more for your girl to be that turned on, but I was about to explode in the back seat of that car.

It was sensory overload, and I knew the moment I got home I was going to be destroyed in every single way and love every depraved second of it.

When we got home, I stripped off, needing a shower. The Unicorn joined me a few minutes later. Being this naked with someone you only just met can be a fucking scary thing. But it wasn't with him.

He pulled me into his chest, and we kissed.

Slow and passion-filled—my most favorite kiss of all.

The water cascaded around us, and with the lights off, it felt almost dreamlike. Like a scene out of one of my books.

This wasn't my life.

This didn't happen to me.

I wasn't accustomed to a man hugging me and kissing me this way. He was rough yet gentle. He was reckless yet careful.

And he was always respectful.

I couldn't keep up.

I was losing a race I didn't even know I was running.

I had long given up on the idea that this type of man existed, so to have this now, I was slowly becoming addicted to the taste.

Each kiss grew.

Each touch lingered.

He was everywhere, yet I wanted more.

And I knew in that precise moment…I wanted to keep him.

My heart hurt because it was not prepared for yet another heartbreak. But I didn't care.

I wanted this man more than I needed air to breathe.

We went into the bedroom, and what he did next…oh, be still my iniquitous heart.

He bent me over his lap, and with my ass poised high, he slapped me—so fucking hard.

Each time, it was harder.

Each time, I died a small death.

He asked if I wanted more.

If I wanted it harder.

And each question was answered with a yes.

This wasn't something we spoke about. We were just in sync with what we wanted. My body responded to his. And his to mine.

I was so turned on by this stage. I don't remember the last time I was this wet.

So the question is, why is he called The Unicorn?

Yes, it *is* what you're all thinking. You wouldn't be reading this book if it wasn't. You're all my dirty little monsters, which is why you'll understand.

He *was* one of a kind. Of course he was. You've read what a rarity he was.

But The Unicorn's horn was the biggest, the longest, the hardest thing I had ever seen, and it was about to fuck me into next week and do so with a shameless smile.

And I was so here for it.

This was it—make or break.

He established early on that he was in control, and when he lay on top of me and fucked the ever-living shit out of me, I was a goner.

I didn't stand a chance.

We had sex unlike strangers.

We fit.

Although I was submerged in everything that was The Unicorn, I molded to his body and his to mine.

I was little.

He was big.

Two pieces of a puzzle we were still unsure of what the picture was.

He kissed me.

He restrained me as he spat the filthiest things into my ear.

I had to close my eyes because his eye contact was almost too much.

I felt him breaking every part of me—both literally and figuratively.

Again, his touches were rough but gentle.

He was a lover who read their partner and watched for their cues to what made them cry harder. Or elicit a string of profanity as they were robbed of any other words.

And then he continues to push until you're straddling the line of pleasure and pain.

Skin to skin.

His body warmed mine.

I was slipping into an abyss, but I would happily fall because he was more to me in that one night than the men prior to me were in months.

Years.

The sex lasted for what felt like a very long time.

Never did I grow bored.

Never did I feel like it was too much.

On the contrary, I wanted more.

But I didn't realize how much more was headed my way…

I woke to a kiss on the shoulder and a "Good morning, gorgeous."

The Unicorn had stayed over.

A first for me because it had been a long time since I shared my bed with a man.

Someone shouldn't look this incredibly hot in the morning.

But in the morning light, The Unicorn was even more incredible.

He wore stubble the way I like it.

And his eyes were that vibrant color when one first wakes.

He smiled.

I died.

I needed to slap some sense into myself because I was waiting for the inevitable yawn and overhead stretch before the infamous words of, "Thanks for a fun night, but I gotta go."

I braced for it, but it never came.

The Unicorn did, however…numerous times.

How could the sex be getting better?

This was impossible.

We spent the entire day hanging out, watching TV, and having mind-blowing sex.

Repeat.

Just when I thought he couldn't outdo himself, he went and did…*that*.

It was a first.

It's not a myth, ladies.

I made a mess.

Curious?

It starts with an S and ends with a quirt.

He was so not sorry that he was the cause of such a mess.

He carried me into the bedroom, and I remember feeling utterly safe in his arms. And that, to me, is the most important factor in any partnership.

Feeling safe and loved.

The Unicorn stayed that night too.

We spoke about everything and anything. Again, I was shocked at how natural things felt.

Even when he didn't stay on his side of the bed, and I ended up on the edge, I loved feeling him close by.

I didn't realize I had missed sleeping beside someone, and then I appreciated that even when I had, that person may as well have been sleeping in the next room.

The Unicorn was the perfect sleeping partner.

He didn't snore.

He slipped his arm under my pillow and cradled me into his chest. But when he turned, he ensured I turned with him as it was my turn to be the big spoon.

Slipping my arm under his, I ran my fingers over his chest.

Or along his upper shoulder and neck.

He would sigh and cuddle closer to me.

It warmed my heart.

He told me he had walls up, but asleep, his guard lowered, and who I saw was someone I wanted in my bed every night.

There was such a gentle streak to him, but in no way did I mistake that as weakness. Perhaps like a wounded animal who fought his entire life to survive. And when he was shown kindness, he didn't know how to respond as he wasn't accustomed to someone being nice to him without wanting something in return.

I didn't want anything in return.

All I wanted was him.

Love ♡ HardER

The Unicorn spent the weekend, and come Monday, reality set in, and it was time to part ways.

He left and promised to text when he got back home.

This was the moment of truth.

I tried to keep busy at work, but the ghosts of my exes wouldn't leave me be.

Sparkles and Mötley assured me he was different.

I wasn't holding my breath.

But when my phone lit up with a text, I was proven wrong.

It was The Unicorn asking how work was.

I needed to chill the fuck out.

This didn't mean anything.

He was a nice guy.

It didn't mean he wanted to see me again.

Mötley had the wine and snacks ready when I came home from work.

She wanted to know it all.

And I told her.

Every single thing from start to finish. I needed to express it out loud for fear I had dreamed the entire thing.

She swooned and stuck to her first impression of him, that he wasn't going anywhere.

It's remarkable what others see when looking at you.

She told me how he would look at me when I spoke, and he smiled. She said he never stopped smiling. I often wonder what he thought.

He called me that night, and we spoke for about six hours.

The next night, the same thing happened.

My friends were impressed and wanted their own unicorn.

I didn't know when I would see him again, but it was okay. I liked that we talked well into the night. There never was a pause or a dull moment.

The Unicorn was back at work the next day, so I assumed I wouldn't see him until he was off next. But he texted me and said he was thinking of coming over.

I was confused.

Did he mean now?

He had to drive out of his way to see me as his house is closer to work than mine is. But he said he wanted to see me.

And I wanted to see him.

So before I knew it, The Unicorn was standing on my doorstep, looking a dirty dream—I mean that in the literal sense as The Unicorn gets his hands dirty in all components of life.

He ate, showered, and then we went to bed, where he did things to me that were illegal in at least ten different countries.

There is usually one thing that your partner does or says that makes you go weak at the knees, and for me, it's spoken words, of course. When barking orders at me, I would rebel (no surprise), and what he would say to me, I just wanted to defy him even harder because, oh my lord…

The words he spoke, although simple, left me a salivating mess.

"Do what you're told."

The moment he said those words, I did the opposite as I knew what followed.

He'd slap my ass.

He'd order me to spit in his mouth.

He'd pull my hair.

He'd choke me.

He'd talk dirty.

He'd eat me out in a way that had me wondering, where the fuckity fuck did he learn that?

He'd fuck me into submission.

And then we'd fall asleep close together, his gentle breathing lulling me to sleep.

This was our routine for a week.

And I was becoming hooked.

So were my friends who loved The Unicorn.

They wanted to hang out as his energy was addictive. I loved the way he engaged with them.

I spoke to his family on the phone early on.

He made it clear I wasn't a secret; something which was a culture shock for me. He often said his friends didn't believe I was real. That I was The Unicorn's imaginary girlfriend.

The more time I spent with him, the more I liked.

This was bad.

My heart prepared for battle.

He was beyond handsome, and I often looked at him when he was distracted. The way he would use his left hand for some things but his right for others, or the cute little gaps between his teeth. Or the heart shape at the end of his nose.

I admired all the things he probably overlooked. He was simply beautiful.

Usually, someone needs a muse to be inspired, and The Unicorn quickly became mine. I mentioned how Switzerland was on the cover of *LOVE HARD*, and his tattoos were a distinguishing feature. He never wanted any notoriety. He was just happy to do something important to me.

I then had an idea.

I asked The Unicorn if perhaps he would like to do a cover with me because even though I had no idea where this was headed, I would always remember him as the boy who was different from the rest.

He seemed hesitant at first because perhaps his confidence was shattered due to someone not loving him how he deserved. But he said he would do it for me, and just when I thought he couldn't surprise me any more than he already had, he told me he wanted to get a tattoo…of a unicorn.

I had given him a list of the names Mötley and I had come up with for him as I had told him I wanted to write about us because this story was so unlike anything I've ever told. The Unicorn was the first name I thought of, but usually, one associates unicorns with glitter and five-year-old girls' birthday parties.

But he laughed and said what did I like best. I said The Unicorn because that's what you are—you're my unicorn. You really are one of a kind.

So he stated, "The Unicorn it is, then."

So he was known as The Unicorn from that day forward.

So the tattoo touched me in so many ways.

We searched for the perfect image, and his sister sent him one that summed him up perfectly—he was a dark horse beneath that unicorn skin. And the ink he got reflected this.

The Unicorn had a darkness too.

It sang to mine.

We understood one another well because perhaps our pasts were parallel.

Love hurt us both, and when love hurts you over and over again when all you've done is try, one cannot help but be one with the darkness when the light refuses to shine.

He opened up more about his past, and I understood why he was the way he was. His walls were erected to protect himself, and whenever I did something for him, it left him out of sorts. For someone to receive the bare minimum and then to receive more than they have, it confuses them and leaves them questioning why.

It hurt my heart.

I didn't want to make him uncomfortable, but I do things for the people I care for because seeing them happy makes me happy.

And I wanted to see The Unicorn smile because when he did, it was beautiful.

But he was still my Rubik's Cube as I was forever second-guessing him.

Perhaps when I got too close, he retreated.

I didn't push because when someone pushes me, I do the complete opposite, which is ironically also a part of The Unicorn's DNA.

He would message every morning and night before he went down into his hole for work, and then the moment he was above ground, he would text and tell me he was coming over.

We fell into his pattern so easily.

Mötley was convinced he was moving in.

I had delegated his own drawer, and he had his own toothbrush. I just wanted to make things easier for him. He never asked me for one single thing. All he wanted was to spend time together.

We did everything and anything.

I often asked him to write something for me as he was left-handed, which is my weakness. We all have a kink, and mine is a left-handed man. So when he spanked me, choked me, or slipped his fingers inside me with his left hand, it drove me wild.

He didn't know this, but remember, I pay attention to the things that most people don't. I don't miss the small things the universe drops into my lap. But The Unicorn wasn't something small. He was soon becoming a big part of my world. It felt as though he was always a part of it.

He was close to perfect.

Was he?

Absolutely not.

But who is?

He didn't make me angry.

He didn't annoy me—much.

We had been in one another's space since we met.

He was thoughtful.

Considerate.

He was kind.

I liked being beside him in silence.

He calmed me.

But my head started doing that thing it does when things are calm.

I began to self-sabotage.

I scrutinized.

I looked for things that weren't there. But I was convinced they were. I just wasn't looking hard enough.

My heart couldn't be happy. It forgot how to beat without pain.

There had to be a catch.

There always is.

And I found it when someone inboxed me the moment I posted The Unicorn on my socials.

It was such a rookie move on my behalf as this has happened before. But I wanted to believe he was different.

She told me to check his phone.

My stomach dropped.

Not again.

He was sleeping beside me. And I looked at him. Memorizing who this man was because I promised to never see him again if history was about to repeat itself.

If he proved to be like the others, then I would be stronger this time.

No second chances.

No second best.

I asked him why this woman had told me to check his phone.

He took a little while to reply.

Did I sense deception?

Was he trying to come up with a credible story?

I felt sick.

He explained the situation.

It only made me feel worse.

Sparkles told me something which stuck; she said you don't really know a person or the foundation of your relationship until your first fight.

And although very early days, I could see that The Unicorn cared.

He never raised his voice.

He never avoided my questions.

However, the more he explained, the angrier I got.

Trigger after trigger slapped me in the face, and my heart was screaming at me to abort this mission before we got hurt again.

I didn't understand why he chose to do what he did.

Perhaps he didn't feel what I thought he did.

Perhaps he was just waiting for the next best thing to come along.

Or perhaps I'd never find anyone to see me for who I really was.

Tears welled, but no more.

It's hard being mad when the cause is right beside you, trying to make amends.

I needed space away from him.

It was too much.

I wanted to believe him.

But I had believed the others, which is why I didn't believe him.

They lied.

They all do.

They may have meant it at the time, but it was never enough in the end.

I left the room and sat in my sanctuary, where words saved me time and time again.

He called out to me. But each attempt to remedy things just made me feel worse.

It felt as though every single ex who lay dead and buried rose from the dead, haunting me with their memories.

I knew love had hurt me, but I didn't realize how much so until now. I had an amazing man putting in the time and the effort, and here I was, crying over something that didn't exist.

The harder I tried to see reason, the harder it got to breathe.

Feelings of rejection and self-worth threatened to strangle me because this would end the way it always had.

Why was he different?

I was the chaos.

He was the calm.

But he would never tame my storm…no one ever would.

He would often mention that after some months, he would be leaving the state, even the country.

It was Switzerland all over again.

Was I just someone to fill in the time until he left?

He came into my office to see if I was okay. I could see it all over his beautiful face that he was upset.

Never angry, however.

He never got mad.

He asked if I wanted him to leave.

I didn't know what I wanted other than to stop feeling this way.

Eventually, I went back to bed, where he lay awake.

This was the first time the silence between us spoke volumes.

He asked me to talk to him.

But I didn't know what to say.

He had told me who this woman was.

And I hated that he had done what he had.

Was it terrible?

Yes and no.

Could I move on from this hiccup early on?

I honestly didn't know.

We lay face to face, The Unicorn watching me closely, just how he always did.

He asked me to kiss him.

I gave him a quick kiss on those lush lips.

He said, "More."

I did.

"More."

Again, more was had.

"More."

One final time.

He sighed, clearly saddened he had caused me pain.

He then said something that made me want to cry new tears. "Come lay on my chest."

There is something so comforting about that.

Heart to heart.

Skin to skin.

But I couldn't.

I needed to slam the brakes on this because I said the one thing to The Unicorn that summed up how I was feeling.

"You're going to break my heart."

But I guess, in some ways, he already had.

I didn't sleep much.

So when the morning light broke through the curtains, I arose, and autopilot kicked in. I got ready for the day while The Unicorn slept.

I left him in bed when I went to work.

He asked for a kiss.

He knew things were amiss.

I tried hard to be understanding. But another woman being involved so early on just had me wanting to forget we had ever met.

He texted me throughout the day.

His messages were heartfelt.

They were honest and raw.

He apologized and could see why I was upset. He wanted to make things work.

Message after message was sent, each one expressing himself in ways no man has ever done for me before.

I wish I could share them with you, dear reader, but they are something personal between The Unicorn and me.

But believe me when I say, those messages changed everything.

He called many times.

He wouldn't roll over and let this die.

He chased me because perhaps he knew I ran when scared.

When I replied, I wrote down my feelings, which I could not express verbally.

Most men would have run the other way because I didn't hold back. Although he had owned up, it didn't make things all right.

I needed him to know that I wasn't one to suppress my emotions. And if he wasn't okay with that, then we would never work. I also didn't appreciate a comment he made about our age differences. So I decided to also touch on that because why the hell not?

I didn't expect him to reply.

I figured he'd run away like all the others had when I was being "difficult."

But he didn't.

"Can I call you please?"

This was a man fighting *for* me, not fighting with me.

I was torn.

But in the end, my heart won.

He called, and we spoke for a long time.

I could hear the sincerity in his voice.

We have to make mistakes to learn from them, and The Unicorn learned that I am stubborn and to never mistake my kindness for weakness.

And I learned that The Unicorn fights for what he wants, and it was apparent…that he wanted me.

It wasn't our first fight, per se. But it was a moment that revealed a different side to The Unicorn.

Ironically, the other woman brought The Unicorn and me closer together as we had "the talk."

He was mine.

I was his.

And we would work everything else out along the way.

It was hard to remember that we had only been seeing one another for such a short amount of time because we just fit.

But we needed to slow it down.

It seemed like the sensible thing to do.

But that idea lasted for about a minute.

I was so drawn to him because he was authentic. But being with him showed me just how broken by love I truly was because I was constantly waiting for the dreaded "but." I was putting my faith and trust in yet another man, and we all know how that ended.

I wanted to believe him, but when something is a little too good to be true, it usually is.

But my friends, once again, swooped in and were my voice of reason when mine was on a sabbatical. They said no man puts the time and effort in as The Unicorn had if they didn't like you.

The Unicorn himself had said the same thing.

Let this be a lesson for us all—if a man wants a woman, he is never too busy. He makes the time to see her, regardless of what he's doing, and The Unicorn had proven that to me time and time by working the long days and hours he did, only to drive those extra miles to spend time with me.

If a man wants a woman, he makes the effort—period.

And The Unicorn was the only man who put the effort in and continued to do so. Yes, a man will chase at the beginning, but when they get what they want, most will retreat because the chase is over.

Men like the chase. When we make it too easy for them, the challenge is no longer there, and they move on to the next best thing that catches their attention; a little like dogs chasing a new chew toy.

I wondered why this wasn't the case with The Unicorn.

That's when Mötley said something that stuck. She said you *are* the next best thing. I can see that. And so can he.

I was so damaged by past loves that I no longer remembered that love can be simple too.

Yes, it's fucking painful and, most times, leaves you questioning *everything*. But sometimes, love can be kind. The type of love that makes us fight for our HEAs.

And I was soon realizing that I would fight for The Unicorn because he had done so for me.

We knew we had amazing sexual chemistry.

And that we vibed when together.

But the test was when we were apart.

And that was soon to be put into play because it was time for reality to kick in.

Often, those refer to the new beginnings of a relationship as the honeymoon period, where their new beau can do no wrong and the ick is nonexistent.

But with The Unicorn, it never felt like that because it always felt like we had known one another for longer than we had.

However, I was interested to see how our separation would pan out.

I honestly was waiting for the other shoe to drop the entire time. There was no way I had found a man who was funny and kind, incredibly thoughtful, so goddamn hot, and could fuck me into a coma.

This sort of man does not exist in real life.

The Unicorn was book boyfriend material, which is why I was constantly waiting for something to go wrong.

Not the most optimistic way to view things, but was it realistic—yes.

The time we shared together was nothing short of amazing, so when he kissed me goodbye, I wondered if this was a memory in the making. If it was, I would be okay with the fact because The Unicorn was the first man in a very long time to treat me with respect and care.

I spoke to my friends who could relate to it. It saddened me that we were all traumatized by love in one way or another.

I went about my day, not expecting much, so when The Unicorn texted me, asking how my day was, I wondered if this was a trick question.

I replied, waiting for the "it's been fun…but…"

But it never came.

We spoke just as we did when together.

He called every single day, and I can say that until this day, not a day has passed when he hasn't called. We have spoken every day since we met.

The Unicorn was slowly penetrating the walls I had erected around my heart, and I knew my original thought that he would break it was soon becoming true.

He was the type of man I wrote about—complete alpha. Stubborn but kind. Incredibly loyal, but wasn't afraid to tell it how it was. A wounded MC who still liked to pull his girl close after he fucked her until she forgot her own name.

He was the epitome of every bad boy I penned, but he wasn't fiction.

He was real.

And I wanted him.

His work schedule was crazy busy, but he made it work as best he could, again coming to see me at the expense of sleep and doing the things he needed to do.

He called one early morning after his shift, stating he was coming over.

He never asked.

He did what he wanted.

And I loved that about him.

He was as headstrong as me.

He was determined.

And he was so fucking bossy.

Be still my heart…

But I told him I had a million and one things to do.

The disappointment in his voice touched me. It had been a few days since we had seen one another. Could it be he missed me?

Because I sure as shit missed him.

And this, boys and girls, is the "oh fuck me" moment.

We didn't see one another for a week, and history has proven that in dating time, that could equate to someone getting married and divorced in that short time span.

A lot can happen.

And what happened between The Unicorn and I was that he called me on the drive to work every day. He never missed a day. We spoke about everything. He became my voice of reason when I was ready to throat punch someone. And I loved listening to him. He could read his shopping list to me, and I would happily listen.

I knew I was falling for him, and I was powerless to stop it.

He just fit into my world, and I guess I did the same for him.

How did this happen?

I wasn't lucky in love.

This sort of stuff doesn't happen in real life. It especially doesn't happen to me.

But the Unicorn was ready to chase each time I wanted to run.

The morning he came over after not seeing one another for a week is my favorite memory to this day. I was asleep as he had worked all through the night and drove over an hour to my house after he had finished his shift.

He came in quietly, crawled into bed with me, and hugged me into his chest. He kissed my neck as he hugged me so tight, and the gesture touched me in so many ways.

I told him I missed him.

And he said he missed me.

I don't know what it is about a hug.

Perhaps the feeling of being safe in your lover's arms.

Or maybe it was because The Unicorn wasn't overly affectionate, something I had to adjust to because I am the complete opposite, and when my partner doesn't replicate the touchy feels, I wonder if maybe they've checked out.

When speaking to Sparkles and Mötley about this, I realized I am like this because past relationships were based heavily on the physical. I am accustomed to being validated through smutty comments or via sex, but it wasn't that way with The Unicorn.

However, it still played on my mind that maybe this was a one-sided deal.

If anyone were to ask what my favorite memory is of him and me, it would be that hug.

We spent more time together, our connection growing, yet I forever second-guessed everything.

I had the most amazing man in front of me, and all I could do was look behind. It was beyond frustrating, but I was damaged, and I didn't expect anything different this time.

But I really tried.

When I wanted to give up, my friends would reason with me all the beautiful things The Unicorn did to show me that he was all in. They were all crushing on him too because they loved me, and to see a man treat their girl the way he was, they couldn't help but get a little swoony whenever he was around.

The saying rings true that best friends will be as involved in your relationship as you are because they never asked how I was without asking how he was too.

He was wedging his way into our worlds, and although this all sounds like every girl's dream, deep down, it soon turns into my nightmare.

There is a line I wrote in *LOVE HARD*, and looking back now, I wonder if this was a sign from the universe because if only I knew.

I've learned that good men are like unicorns. Everyone talks about them, but no one actually sees them.

How I was eating my words because I had found my unicorn. I had managed to somehow stumble across a man who was only ever spoken about but never seen, yet there was something missing.

Plot twist?

Yeah, it seems I like to catch myself unawares also.

I don't know what it was, but it sometimes felt as though he was present but not. Yes, he made the effort to see me, but when he did, it sometimes felt he was somewhere else.

A friend made a passing comment that maybe I was more into him than he was into me. I pondered on this for a long while. She said try it.

Take note of who is more affectionate.

Pay attention to who holds whose hand first.

Or who initiates the first touch.

And I did.

Can you guess who it was?

Yes, it was me.

For someone who takes pride in seeing the small things that others might not, I had totally dropped the ball.

That sinking feeling returned, and no matter how many times my friends tried to reassure me, I just couldn't shake this déjà vu away.

The closer I paid attention to it, the more I saw that I was the one who instigated the hand-holding or the hugs, while he was the one who initiated sex.

Touch is my love language, and now that I realize I'm the one who is touching, I want to stop it immediately because I feel like a fool.

Was this a me problem?

He had told me he was guarded.

But so was I.

The more I thought about this, the more it festered. Until I do what I do best…I ran.

Not literally, but I took a step back.

I needed to view whatever this was objectively and dissect it. This is the advice I would give any friend, so it was time I took my own advice because The Unicorn could break me, and I knew if he did, there would be no coming back this time.

I had opened my heart, and now I was wondering if maybe I should have been a little wiser with my choices. Not with The Unicorn, but rather, slamming on the brakes and edging into this new adventure with caution.

Deep down, I knew these were my insecurities pulling me into every direction and my heart going into self-preservation mode. I wish I could stop it, that I could slap my own ass. But it felt as though I had forgotten how to be treated how every woman deserves.

The happiness was forever being overshadowed by doubt, and I was watching myself destroy something that was nothing but beautiful.

Trust the overthinker when they tell you that they like you, for they have thought of every reason not to.

This would be the time that any other man would run, but The Unicorn never did.

If I went quiet, lost in my head, he would always be there, asking what I was thinking. He never gave up. He pressed until I told him, and for someone who is an avoidant, it was hard not to do what comes intrinsically and that was destroy everything and leave chaos in your wake.

But The Unicorn stayed.

Not once did he want a break.

Not once did he go back on his word.

I was the one who kept looking for something that wasn't there.

I cried to Mötley many times, frustrated at myself. I wanted to stop being such an idiot and accept this for what it was. The Unicorn and I were more together than we were apart and when we were apart, we were still talking.

So what was the issue here?

Me...

Simple.

I was scared.

As much as I hate to admit it, I was fucking petrified. Petrified of fucking this up.

My exes had always made me feel as though I was to blame for whatever went wrong, and it seemed as though this rationale tarnished this new relationship by my hand.

Angel, Sparkles, and Mötley were always in my corner and would support me no matter what, but this was one thing they all wouldn't budge from. The Unicorn wasn't like the other guys I dated. Hell, he wasn't like most guys if we were to be fair. He was an anomaly. He was someone I was forever attempting to decode, but in the end, I saw him for who he was.

He was mine, and he wasn't going anywhere.

I was the one who tried to sabotage us, but he was the one who promised me time and time again that it would be okay.

And he was right…

But please don't tell him that.

The Unicorn's birthday was soon approaching, and true to his star sign, he was the typical Cancer.

Although he didn't believe in astrology, he still humored me.

When he said, "It's 11:11," something which I say daily, I wanted to kiss his face and never stop.

He did things that showed me he listened.

On the other hand, I don't listen, which is why I wanted to throw him a birthday party, which I knew may not go down well.

The Unicorn made clear early on that he didn't like gifts. He didn't like people making a fuss. I didn't want to force him into doing anything he wasn't comfortable with, but it was his birthday, and I wanted it to be special because it was the first one we were to share.

And he was special to me.

I told him about my plans, certain he would politely decline. But he didn't. He said he would love it.

I went on to plan a small gathering. It gave my friends a chance to meet the man I was spending my time with.

I didn't want to overwhelm him, but I wanted to buy him something special, something he could look back on and always remember this day.

It goes without saying, unicorn gifts were bought, as was a watch that I wanted to see on that inked wrist. But as mentioned earlier, The Unicorn likes to drift over to my side of the bed, so to prevent any confusion on whose side was whose, I got our names embroidered on pillows and placed them on our sides.

The stage was set, and when The Unicorn arrived and saw his party in full swing, I worried I had done too much. I didn't want him to be uncomfortable, but putting myself in his shoes, I understood why he may feel a little uneasy.

He mingled, but he seemed ill at ease.

Was it too much?

Cake was eaten, and again, I didn't know if The Unicorn wanted this night to end already. He wasn't ungrateful, but he just seemed uneasy the entire time. Our guests left as I had planned a night out. However, I was wondering if perhaps we should just stay home instead.

I was getting ready in my room when The Unicorn entered. It was the first time we were alone all night.

He looked at me, and again, the Rubik's Cube presented itself.

I thought I had done something wrong.

I then remembered the pillows.

I asked The Unicorn to turn them over, and when he saw them, I knew I hadn't. I realized that perhaps this was just a lot for a man who had never really experienced a birthday like this before.

He hugged me tight and thanked me for everything I had done. Although he said it was too much, he appreciated it immensely.

There was so much emotion in that embrace.

We went in separate cars to the club, and he texted me, thanking me once again for the gifts. He also asked if I wanted him to wait outside for me.

This man was the perfect gentleman.

I walked up the stairs and saw him standing at the top. He didn't see me at first, so I took this moment to observe the man stealing my heart.

But how can something be stolen when you want it to be had?

He looked beyond hot in ripped black jeans and a white shirt. The watch filled me with a sense of joy, and I could see he wore it with pride. He was tall, big, and the hottest guy in the club, and he was all mine.

Goes without saying he was greeted with a kiss.

Although The Unicorn and I had our first date in a club, this was different. Then, we were strangers, but now, we were something else entirely.

I wondered what type of partner The Unicorn was when it came to going out with friends.

Was he happy to kiss at the start of the night only to find one another at the end of the night? Did he want to do his thing with the boys?

I didn't know.

This was new territory for me.

So I let him lead.

Wherever I was…he found me.

When he didn't, he made sure that he did.

He always watched to see where I was.

When our gazes locked, he would smile and "reel me in," as he danced to the god-awful music.

He was never far away, but he gave me space.

I liked that he was always close by.

He held my hand.

He hugged me.

He kissed me.

His eyes were always searching for me.

There never was a doubt of who belonged to whom.

And in case I ever forgot, he bent down and assertively stated, "You're mine and no one else's."

He only had eyes for me.

Never once did I feel crowded.

I felt safe. Assured. Something I hadn't felt in a very long time with a man.

He was my protector, and I was falling so irrevocably hard for him.

I had crossed the point of no return.

The chemistry was rampant and pressed up against a wall, it was for all to see when a passerby stopped and commented how hot we looked together and that we should hook up. The Unicorn's quick wit came into play when he replied, "We're married."

We were apart for a little while before I'd receive a message asking where I was. And to come find him. Or he'd come find me.

If things got heated as they do when drunk, he would level me with those eyes and ask I didn't leave. Cinderella was about to lose her glass slipper, but I stayed because I couldn't say no to him. But I was ready to leave soon.

He said he liked having a woman who put him in his place because I did that often.

All was going well with the night, surprisingly without a hitch.

Now, dear reader, were you paying attention to what I said earlier about a man wanting a woman and what said man will do to express his wants to his woman?

A friend was in a situationship, and we all know how those end. I *was* in one, remember?

The Unicorn had tried alongside me to help her see reason, but you can't force someone to do anything. And my friend just wouldn't listen. She was certain he would come around, but it had been six months, and there was no light at the end of the tunnel.

The situationship ended up at the same club as us, and The Unicorn decided to talk to him. But that went down like a bag of dicks. The Unicorn was attempting to protect my friend from heartache, but he also saw what it was doing to me because I hated seeing her in pain.

The Unicorn was trying to be the good guy, but in turn, things were about to turn fucking messy, and our HEA was about to be turned on its axis. Once again, I was left questioning what the actual fuck?

Love ♡ HardER

The Unicorn's birthday was fun.

We spent the next day together, hanging out and keeping a low profile. It was nice. I loved lying in bed with him, watching movies and kissing because that kissing would turn to mind-blowing sex followed by cuddles.

I loved laying with my ear pressed to his chest, listening to his heartbeat. It often calmed me. His arms were quickly becoming my favorite place to sleep as there was one thing I noticed.

He was becoming more and more affectionate.

He would touch my face.

Over my legs.

He would ask me to cuddle him in bed after he cuddled me for hours.

Could it be those impenetrable walls were slowly coming down?

His touches were becoming more frequent and almost second nature in a sense. My theory of him not instigating contact was now obsolete.

As I paid closer attention to the way we interacted, I realized that The Unicorn *was* affectionate all along—in his own way, and as we spent more time together, the touches, the hand-holding, all the stuff that I was questioning came naturally.

And that's how any relationship should be. Nurture it, and it will grow.

The more time spent with him, the more I liked. He was unlike any man I had ever met.

I trusted him, which was something I hadn't done in a very long time.

For the first time in my life, things in my love life were calm.

And of course, that's when I lowered my guard and got sucker punched straight in the heart.

Why is it when you're happy, the unhappy come out in droves and decide to shit on your happiness? I guess the saying rings true—misery loves company.

The situationship I spoke of, he mentioned to my friend that he saw The Unicorn in a compromising position with another girl and that he was worried for me as The Unicorn was perhaps a fuckboy beneath his magical skin.

I was quiet for a very long time, unsure how to process this nugget of information because what in the ever-living fuck?

When did this supposedly happen?

The Unicorn was with me for the majority of the night, and when he wasn't, he was texting to see where I was.

But trigger after trigger came out of hiding, and I couldn't help but feel like they were just lying dormant, waiting to smack me in the face with "I told you so."

I didn't know how to feel. I didn't want to believe this as true, but was I being naive? Was The Unicorn just like everyone else?

I sent him a message saying we needed to talk.

Goes without saying, a restless night's sleep was had.

He called me early the following morning on his way to work. I could hear the concern in his tone. I relayed what I was told, and then the floor was his.

He denied this ever happened, but I asked why would the situationship lie? In hindsight, this was a stupid question, considering he was stringing my friend along for months, but was this the "but" I was looking for?

The Unicorn's character was being attacked, and he could have walked away at any moment, but he didn't.

He never did.

He brought up some very valid points, but in the end, it all came down to trust.

This was the moment of truth.

Did I trust The Unicorn?

He had a solid explanation, but anyone can concoct a story to cover their guilty ass. It was the way The Unicorn handled the situation that made my mind up.

He didn't yell.

He didn't beg.

He simply told it how it was, and if I didn't believe him, then it was on me. He asked me to look back on the evening and make my own mind up.

Who was I to believe?

The situationship who had been nothing but a lying asshole?

Or the man who continued to prove himself time and time again? The man who always held my hand when I wanted to run. The man who wasn't afraid to say sorry when he fucked up. Or stick to his beliefs and never back down.

There was never a decision to make because I realized I would always choose The Unicorn. He will always be my first and last choice because I was his.

Again, irony, as a situation that could have ended our relationship only seemed to strengthen this connection, which continued to grow.

We have faced other challenges after this. I need to show the good and the bad because it wasn't all hearts and roses.

I wish I knew why we, at times, seem to drift apart. Teething issues in a relationship, perhaps? Things would be going so well, and then something would happen, and I began to question why the fuck I was doing this to myself—again.

He did things that frustrated me, like falling asleep on the couch and not coming to bed. After speaking to many friends about the fact, however, it was apparent this pet hate was shared by many, so I felt a little less crazy when I wanted to kick him in the shin.

But he never annoyed me. It was strange because, in my past relationships, I needed space quite often. Even early on. But it was different with The Unicorn. Perhaps it was because we both saw the importance of communicating with the other.

He often said he was tired of fighting. He fought his entire life. He didn't want to fight anymore.

It touched me.

Such honesty is rare.

As is growth.

He was wonderful to my nieces and instantly made an effort to be a part of their lives, so much so that them calling him uncle came naturally.

It became clear early on that The Unicorn was a protector. For someone who wasn't accustomed to such treatment from their partner, my pride initially pushed him away. I didn't need a man to protect me. I had done just fine protecting myself all these years. Heartache had taught me this.

So when he wanted to shield me from harm, I refused.

I could look after myself.

The Unicorn didn't push. Maybe one day I'll need protecting.

If I do, I know who will always be two steps behind me to catch me if I fall.

We fell into a routine quickly. It was innate.

We just fit.

Like when I cuddled him from behind and knew every curve to his muscled chest. His arms would hold me tight. Or the way he would order me to bend over so he could slap my ass. Or often, catch me unawares and slap it when I walked past.

The way he would always find my hand, regardless of the circumstances.

Or the way he would glance at me and I could read him with a single look.

He was becoming my everything, and I was powerless to stop it.

Sex between us had always been intense, but as time grew, so did feelings, and that's when the best sex is had.

I would wake to him kissing my neck from behind and whispering what he wanted me to do as he worked his hand down the front of my sleep shorts. Or slapping my behind.

With just a touch, he would get me so turned on. But this was a new level of desire.

Sex with the right person can be phenomenal. But sex with the person you love…god damn. You don't stand a chance, and that's when I realized that I was in love with The Unicorn.

I still hadn't told him my feelings. I mean, when is the right time to drop such a life-changing event such as this?

There never really is a "right time."

So I didn't force it. I just let it be because I have learned that love should never be forced.

And when you know, you just know.

And I knew when he ordered me to take my favorite seat (on his face) or when we had the type of sex I like (choking, spitting, biting, and obliterating every single inch of me) and he asked if what he was doing was okay, that my heart belonged to the man who changed me in so many ways.

But I don't want you to think it was just the sex that allowed me to reach this epiphany.

It was the way he kissed my forehead or shoulder in the morning when we first woke. Or the way, without fail, he called me baby. The way he held my hand when we crossed the road. Or picked me up and hugged me tight when we hadn't seen one another for a couple of days. The way he would call me amazing before kissing my cheek or the way he spoke to his friends and family about me when I wasn't there. It would always come back to me, and that's so important—what someone says about you when you're not there and what The Unicorn said was filled with nothing but love and admiration.

It was all the small things that equated to this huge picture of I was so fucking screwed.

The dreaded ex was sadly a third wheel at times. The more airtime he gave her, the more it reminded me not to bring up mine because no one likes hearing about their current squeeze's ex. It forever played in the back of my mind that them rekindling was always in the cards.

She was the mother of his children. She would share a bond I never could.

I accepted this for what it was and just needed to trust him.

Trust…there's that word again.

For someone who didn't trust her own shadow, I was coming leaps and bounds.

But it was tough at times, especially when he spoke about her in great detail about something she had done. Unlike my ex, they were still in touch, and when she found out via a mutual friend that he was seeing someone, she had asked so many questions.

I didn't like it.

Why did she care?

My insecurities resurfaced because an ex who shows interest is an ex who cares.

For example, if my ex was the first man to do something noteworthy (highly unlikely), I would never know because I simply do not care.

But she did.

Why?

I can't answer that yet, my besties, because that chapter is yet to come…

But ex aside, I found he could be distant and distracted, and we were forever grappling to see one another because our schedules clashed. I would consult with Mötley, ensuring I wasn't overthinking. She would tell me if I was. When she agreed with me, those were when those feelings of despair would creep in, and I wondered what the point was.

If this was happening so early on, what hope did we have?

I would retreat into my shell. But one night, when things were weird between us, and I didn't know why and started to cry, I knew I was in way over my head.

I hadn't cried over a guy in a long time.

I felt those heavy feelings press down on my chest, and I couldn't breathe.

I didn't want this.

Not again.

I'd prefer to end it now when I could walk away with minimal damage, than later on when I would be totally destroyed.

I hated those days. Those were the times I wanted to end it. I often wonder why I didn't. I guess it's because I wanted to believe that he wasn't doing it intentionally since he gave me so much when he was present.

Did it balance out the scales, however?

Yes, The Unicorn was special, but now that he was spending almost every night in my bed, had the novelty worn off?

I decided to stop assuming and ask him what was going on, and that's when something incredible happened. The Unicorn opened up in ways never before, and I realized that, just like me, he also gets in his head and suppresses his pain.

This had nothing to do with me.

Love, remember, had hurt him too, and he was dealing with it as best he could. And in response, he pushed down his own demons to pacify mine because that was the first time he told me he loved me.

Other beautiful things were said, and I knew then that The Unicorn wasn't going anywhere. He assured me it would be okay and not to worry; he was staying.

And so was I.

We've fought.

We've kissed and made up.

Arguing with him has me realizing how far I've grown when it comes to relationships.

In the past, I would sit on my feelings until they came to a boiling point and I would explode. That's usually the point of no return.

Neither of us wanted to drag out an argument. Yes, we were both stubborn and stuck to our convictions, but once we both said what we wanted, the discussion was over and we always seemed to grow from something which had the potential to tear us apart.

When I'm sad, he makes me happy.

When I'm scared, he protects me.

And the way he holds me tight in the darkness as we lay side by side has me falling in love with him all over again.

I still don't know what our future holds, but so far, we prevailed together because if you don't have communication, trust, and honesty with your partner, then your relationship will eventually fail.

That is one thing I learned firsthand. And I wasn't going to make that mistake again because The Unicorn, I think, just might be my forever.

And now…I can only hope I'm his.

Love ♡ HardER

Artist: Hanze

So there you have it, the unplanned chapter, which is the rawest, most heartfelt thing I've ever written.

My story with The Unicorn is still unraveling, and I hope it continues to write itself for years to come. But what is ahead for him and I, I honestly do not know. I survived the hardships with love and just when I wanted to give up, I found the man who changed everything I thought I knew.

He healed my heart when I thought it was broken beyond repair.

And this is why I needed to include his chapter because I wanted to end this memoir with nothing but love.

I wanted to show you all facets of love.

The good.

The bad.

The ugly.

And the miracle that love is.

I wanted to be as raw as I could. I didn't want to skim around the edges and leave anything out. I also didn't want to shame love because love has the ability to change the world.

It sure as shit has changed mine.

Am I scared to be this vulnerable?

Of course I am.

But I've never been one to let my fears stop me from living because I don't want to look back on this life with regret.

Love has hurt The Unicorn too.

Just as it has me.

Just as it has you.

And we all respond to love in different ways.

That's what makes our stories unique and our own.

So the burning question seems to be…are The Unicorn and I together?

I presented a choose-your-own-adventure-style ending in *LOVE HARD*, but some readers didn't like the fact they didn't have closure.

But, dear reader, my story will forever be changing because my life isn't set in stone; the decisions I make reflect my future, so there will never be an ending as such.

But, the answer is this book you hold in your hands and the cover you see. This cover, very much like *LOVE HARD*, captured a moment in time that will be etched in time forever.

And I love that so much.

Bunny was able to shoot that precise second between The Unicorn and me, which can never be replicated because time is priceless and so are rare moments between two human beings who just…fit.

So does that mean I got my happily ever after?

Time will only tell.

So congratulations, you made it to the end.

Love♡HardER

This story is reflective of millions, but unique because there is only ever one me.

One Ghost.

One Dimples.

One Switzerland.

One Brooklyn.

And of course, one of The Unicorn.

I got my "closure" with Ghost, but realized there is never such a thing with someone who does the damage that he did.

He quit his job and vanished off socials.

Seems he wanted to ghost himself too.

Dimples is still a wound too fresh. I write this without a tear shed because my head and my heart are fighting two different battles. Soon, however, they'll be on the same battlefield, and that's when I will mull over what went wrong.

Maybe one day I will talk to Dimples. But today is not that day.

Brooklyn is honestly a distant memory already. That's an awful thing to admit, but it makes me feel better in a sense because he was never my person.

As for Switzerland, his leaving was one of the hardest things I ever had to deal with. I had to say goodbye to someone I didn't want to say goodbye to.

He taught me so much. But most of all, he helped me heal.

Switzerland did things for me that showed me he cared. He lit candles in his room so it was reflective of my bedroom as he said. He bought me vegan ice cream. He always offered me a blanket, thinking I was cold. He was mindful not to eat meat around me, even though I didn't mind. He always, *always* ensured we touched. He would envelop me in his arms and cuddle me tight.

I don't regret meeting him. He was everything I needed in the short amount of time that we were together.

I always wanted more with him, but he gave me what he could.

But boy number five…The Unicorn. He shattered everything I thought I knew and taught me that the spectrum of colors comes in so many beautiful shades. He taught me that things aren't always what they seem.

I didn't know what *more* was until I met him.

He knocked me onto my ass (not before slapping it, of course, every single day) but ensured he picked me up time and time again.

I don't think he is aware of how special he is.

Well, he is to me anyway.

He is loyal.

Honest.

As I am to him.

I thought all the other men in my past were the real deal, but they weren't. They were a learning curve. A stopover to the final destination…however, I am still not there yet.

But I'm close.

The Unicorn has done the one thing I never thought was possible ever again—he makes me feel safe.

He always makes sure I'm okay.

In his words.

In his gestures.

He does so much to make me happy without even realizing it because that's the sort of man he is. He will always be an ambiguous puzzle that I will never solve. But sometimes there are no answers in life.

Sometimes, things just are.

I often ran from The Unicorn, but I soon learned that, yes, he chased me, but in the end, we always ran side by side; an equal partnership. I was his strength when he needed it, as he was mine.

The pain I still feel from time to time is real.

I am damaged goods.

I'm the first to admit it.

Love♡HardER

Love fucking hurts.

It still does.

I will never heal from some wounds.

But The Unicorn showed me that I wasn't broken by love.

No, I stood up to love when it tried to break me. When I wanted to give up, I persevered because I found men like Ghost, Dimples, Brooklyn, and Switzerland who taught me lessons about myself.

I wasn't a quitter.

I was tenacious.

And I was a motherfucking warrior because I would never, *never* give up.

Trauma doesn't make you stronger. It does what the name suggests; it traumatizes you. It gives you anxiety. And leaves you with trust issues. Trauma forces you to accept feelings you never wanted. Feelings that you don't deserve. These were caused because of someone else's issues. Or in some cases, because of their own trauma.

This wasn't your fault. So I don't agree with the saying what doesn't break you makes you stronger.

You are the one who makes *you* stronger.

Always remember that when life kicks you when you're down.

You are worth so much more than being someone's second choice.

They're not texting you because they don't want to. If they wanted to, they would.

You're confused, and I get it. I am confused most days. But most times, it's simple—the way someone treats you is a reflection of their feelings for you.

It's not your fault if you catch feelings. That's not how the heart loves.

I heard this quote, and it really stuck; a situationship is a relationship to one person and nothing to the other person. If it were mutual, then it would be a relationship.

It's difficult to understand for those who don't love that way, how I love. But we need to remember we're all different. And that's what makes us…us.

Don't let someone be a priority in your life…when you're only an option in theirs.

I may have fallen for the wrong men, but they were wrong for all the right reasons. They taught me what I wanted.

And what I deserved.

And The Unicorn, The Unicorn is my prize.

If I look back on this moment in time and things have changed, then I will always remember that I didn't surrender to love because, besties, love surrendered to me.

In this lifetime and the next…

I found what is meant for me because *I* am the narrator of *my* story. Just as you are of yours. Slay your own dragons; don't wait for Prince Charming to sweep you off your feet. *You* are the one to conquer love, so when your story ends, you can pen those magical words…

She lived happily ever after.

And mean every single word.

Love,

MJ xoxo

Subscribe to my Newsletter: https://tinyurl.com/k3b76tw7
Love Harder Playlist: https://tinyurl.com/j958ad9j

Postface

Congratulations, you made it to the end. You're far braver than some. So, I know what you're thinking…*Is the madness that I just read based on real life?*

And the answer is…abso-fucking-lutely.

About the Author

Monica James spent her youth devouring the works of Anne Rice, William Shakespeare, and Emily Dickinson.

When she is not writing, Monica is busy running her own business, but she always finds a balance between the two. She enjoys writing honest, heartfelt, and turbulent stories, hoping to leave an imprint on her readers. She draws her inspiration from life.

She is a bestselling author in the U.S.A., Australia, Canada, France, Germany, Israel, and The U.K.

Monica James resides in Melbourne, Australia, with her wonderful family, and menagerie of animals. She is slightly obsessed with cats, chucks, and lip gloss, and secretly wishes she was a ninja on the weekends.

Connect with
MONICA JAMES

Facebook: facebook.com/authormonicajames
Twitter: twitter.com/monicajames81
Goodreads: goodreads.com/MonicaJames
Instagram: instagram.com/authormonicajames
Website: authormonicajames.com
TikTok: @authormonicajames
BookBub: bookbub.com/authors/monica-james
Amazon: https://amzn.to/2EWZSyS
Join my Reader Group: http://bit.ly/2nUaRyi
Newsletter: https://tinyurl.com/k3b76tw7

www.ingramcontent.com/pod-product-compliance
Lightning Source LLC
Chambersburg PA
CBHW071909290426
44110CB00013B/1330